Angels with Trumpets

D1329227

Angels with Trumpets

The church in a time of global warming

Paula Clifford

First published in 2009 by
Darton, Longman and Todd Ltd
1 Spencer Court
140–142 Wandsworth High Street
London SW18 4JJ

in association with
Christian Aid
35 Lower Marsh
London SE1 7RL

ISBN 978 0 232 52759 9

A catalogue record for this book is available from the British Library.

Phototypeset by YHT Ltd, London
Printed and bound in Great Britain by
Athenaeum Press, Gateshead, Tyne & Wear

Contents

Introduction

Climate Change and Apocalypse

Blessed is the one who reads aloud the words of the prophecy
... for the time is near.

Revelation 1:3

The last book in the Bible, the Revelation (or Apocalypse) of
St John the Divine, has much in common with the contemporary phenomenon of global warming, which first came
to public attention around 1900 years after John's vision on
the island of Patmos. Both have been distrusted, misused and
misunderstood; both have aroused fears and passions; both
have the potential to inspire movements for good – or not.
Over the centuries many scholars and theologians – not least,
at one point, Martin Luther – have dismissed the Book of
Revelation as unworthy of the biblical canon. And a fair
proportion of people today, within the Church as well as
outside it, have dismissed the climate change debate as mere
scaremongering.

To bring these two things together may seem to some to be
courting disaster, since to use Revelation to encourage action
on climate change is, at first sight, a risky business. What I am
not arguing here is that the world is currently on the brink of

a catastrophe of truly 'biblical' proportions, that we are powerless to prevent and that offers us no hope for the future. And if we look closely enough, Revelation does not tell us that either. Rather, what I want to explore in this book is how John's vision and message can help frame and direct our Christian thinking in the present climate crisis, for that is what it is. So we need to ask ourselves, what does it mean for the Church to speak prophetically, as John did? How best may congregations respond, always bearing in mind John's sometimes damning critique of the seven churches in Revelation 2 and 3? Where does Christian hope for the future lie?

At the same time, we need to examine some of the facts about climate change and, crucially, its various effects on our world and its people. Inevitably this will lead us to reflect on some questions of justice and, indeed, on some of the basic tenets of Christian belief. What does it really mean to love our neighbour in a time of global warming? And as carbon emissions from the rich North wreak havoc with the lives of poor people in the global South, just who is our neighbour? How exactly may the vision of John and the insights of modern theology help us address issues such as these?

This book can be read as a contribution to the theology of climate change or it may be used as a basis for small group study. Each chapter ends with a couple of questions that can be used as discussion starters. My hope is that churches and congregations will be convinced that as Christians we need to take very seriously the various issues associated with climate change. I hope that they will also come to share my view that we need to look hard at how every area of our church lives is affected by the crisis of global warming. And if we can develop some new understanding of the Book of Revelation along the way, so much the better.

Many people have contributed to the thinking that underlies this book. I would especially like to thank the Rt Revd David Atkinson for generously allowing me sight of the manuscript of his book *Renewing the face of the earth*, and the Revd Professor Ian James for helping me make sense of some of the science. But in particular I must thank my colleagues at Christian Aid, both in the UK and overseas, for opening my eyes to the effects of climate change and for allowing me the space to explore the theological issues that they raise. The views expressed in this book should not be seen as necessarily reflecting those of Christian Aid, and responsibility for them and for any errors is mine alone.

Paula Clifford
London, August 2008

Chapter 1

The Time Is Near

Take down de silvah trumpet
Blow yo' trumpet, Gabriel.
Lord, how loud shall I blow it?
Blow it right, calm an' easy
Do not alarm my people
Tell'em to come to judgment.

Spiritual, 'In dat great gittin' up morning'

'Do not alarm my people'

God's advice to Gabriel in that Spiritual is a fair reflection of how most of us would prefer to hear about climate change – 'calm an' easy'. Statements like 'You mustn't frighten people', 'I wouldn't get out of bed in the morning if I believed that', 'Just concentrate on the small things we can all do', are typical of the advice I am offered when I tell people about the rise in global temperatures, the inevitability of disastrous floods and hurricanes, and the urgency of getting governments to act. And a study by the London-based Institute for Public Policy Research in 2006[1] condemned what they called 'alarmist responses', whether from the media or from acknowledged experts such as James Lovelock and Mark Lynas, for distancing people from the problem. Instead they advocated 'persuasive climate-change communications' that would basically make people feel good about undertaking small personal actions in the belief that they are helping to combat global warming.[2]

Now I don't want to discourage anyone from saving energy and doing a hundred and one other things that will lead to a 'greener' lifestyle and make the world a better place. But we are deluding ourselves if we think that altruistic behaviour – voluntarily reducing our personal energy use – is going to catch on in our non-altruistic society, or that if everyone 'does their bit' the problem will be solved. The message of climate change is both profoundly uncomfortable and of the utmost urgency. To try to dilute it, even with the aim of making it more accessible and acceptable to a greater number of people, is to come close to colluding in denial (which we will look at more closely in Chapter 2).

Equally, the 'calm an' easy' message is not a biblical one. The angels in Revelation do not appear to be blowing gently They delivered great 'blasts' (8:13) that were the cue for irresistible forces of nature to take out a third of the earth, sea and stars. Similarly, the events of Revelation are imminent, and there is a note of urgency that runs through even the more temperate letters to the seven churches in chapters 2 and 3.

To water down uncomfortable facts and to shy away from the imminence of destructive events is not part of the

Judaeo-Christian prophetic tradition. While some of the Old Testament prophets certainly started out as reluctant voices – Jeremiah protesting, 'I do not know how to speak, for I am only a boy' (Jer. 1:6); Jonah doing a runner to Tarshish to get away from 'the presence of the Lord' (Jonah 1:3) – they soon make up for it, with Isaiah confronting whole nations with their wickedness and Jonah stirring up Nineveh to immediate repentance.

This is the prophetic heritage of the Christian Church – a call to tell the truth and to tell it with inescapable urgency. But just what is the truth that we are now being called to proclaim?

Climate change: some basic facts

The fragile earth
Just as humans, animals and even fruit depend on their skin to protect them from damage, so planet earth depends on its atmosphere for that human, animal and vegetable life to be sustained. Changes in the atmosphere, however small, will have an inevitable impact on some part of our planet's life. If you imagine a large apple, its skin is equivalent to the earth's atmosphere and, relatively speaking, it is about the same thickness. And while apple skins do their job pretty effectively, we all know how easily the fruit bruises or softens if it is subject to less than ideal conditions.

So the atmosphere, which lends the earth that strange beauty when it is filmed from space, is both vital and fragile. Vital, because without it conditions on earth would rapidly come to resemble those on Venus, our closest relative in the solar system. Fragile, because the balance of its components is so easily disturbed. When scientists measure the concentration of CO_2 in the atmosphere in terms of parts per million, the difference between 300 or 600 parts in every million may seem very slight indeed. In reality it means the difference between life and death.

The beauty of the earth that is celebrated by the Psalmist is rightly seen as God's good creation. It is right that we should marvel at the way in which it all holds together. But that should not blind us to the delicate fragility of those systems, which can all too easily be damaged beyond repair when their make-up is altered.

What's going on?

The earth's climate is constantly and naturally changing due to many factors that need not concern us here. However, one thing which is thought to affect global surface temperatures is the concentration in the atmosphere of 'greenhouses gases' – carbon dioxide in particular and, to a lesser but significant extent, methane.

The natural process known as the 'greenhouse effect', which is essential to life on earth, is well known to most people. In very simple terms, this refers to the process by which the energy from the sun is absorbed by the earth and emitted back into the atmosphere. The infra-red radiation that escapes into space then serves to cool our planet. At the same time, some of that outgoing radiation is absorbed by the atmosphere and trapped, just as the glass roof of a greenhouse traps heat. As the concentration of greenhouse gases increases, the atmosphere thickens so that more radiation is retained. This means that less heat escapes, and the heat in the 'greenhouse' becomes increasingly uncomfortable. Crucially, the delicate balance between incoming and outgoing radiation is disturbed – a balance which is essential to maintaining human life on earth in conditions we can tolerate.

The natural greenhouse effect has begun to look less natural since the 1800s and industrialisation, when the main source of increased greenhouse gases has been the burning of fossil fuels (coal, oil and gas) for transport, industry and power. The rest is due to changing land use, in particular deforestation. For decades this was not a problem: it was the extraordinarily rapid increase in the concentration of greenhouse gases into the atmosphere, particularly carbon dioxide, in the last 40 years or so that led to the present crisis.

At the same time, for commercial, social and political reasons, there was a big increase in deforestation worldwide. We all know that trees absorb CO_2 from the atmosphere through photosynthesis, and while some is released through respiration, some of it stays in the tree as carbon. When trees are felled, the carbon that is released reacts with oxygen in the atmosphere and becomes CO_2. Even more carbon dioxide is released if the trees are burned or left to rot. So the loss of large parts of, say, the Amazon forests, means not only that there are fewer trees to absorb CO_2 but that carbon dioxide has also been emitted along the way. Similarly, countries where trees have been cut down in the course of war, or simply because they are the only source of fuel for poor communities, are making the situation worse. The UNFCCC[3] 13th Conference of Parties held in Bali in December 2007 heard that deforestation was estimated to be responsible for as much as 22 per cent of global carbon emissions, while the Oxford-based Global Canopy Programme, an alliance of leading rainforest scientists reporting a few months earlier, put the figure at 25 per cent.[4]

The Intergovernmental Panel on Climate Change (IPCC), in its Fourth Assessment Report (2007), said this: 'Global greenhouse gas (GHG) emissions have grown since pre-industrial times, with an increase of 70% between 1970 and 2004'.[5] Reluctant as ever to claim absolute certainty, hundreds of scientists and representatives of governments and other organisations say that there is on this point 'high agreement, much evidence', by which they mean 90 to 99 per cent certainty, which is probably enough for most of us. They go on to predict that this trend will continue over the next few decades.

The same report notes that GHG emissions have already reached a level that was not expected for another ten years. In a more recent survey, scientists at the Mauna Loa observatory in Hawaii report that the atmospheric concentration of CO_2 now stands at 387 parts per million (ppm).[6] Between 1970 and 2000, the annual growth rate in concentration was around 1.5 ppm, but since then the average annual rise has been 2.1 ppm. To put this in context, this represents a rise of 40 per cent since the industrial revolution, and it is estimated that if global warming is to remain below an average of 2 degrees centigrade, the concentration of CO_2 must not rise above 450 ppm – although the EU target, the most stringent in the world, currently stands at 550 ppm.

There are two major problems here. The first is that if carbon emissions continue to rise at the current rate, we would have around three decades to turn the situation around, but that rise is not steady, it is accelerating. It is tempting, of course, to point the finger of blame, in particular at economies such as China, which saw its carbon emissions rise by 8 per cent in 2007. But there is no sign of a slow-down in the output of the United States or the European Union either. Added to that, the increase in CO_2 concentration may also indicate that the earth is losing its natural ability to soak up billions of tons of carbon. So climate models assuming that half our emissions will be re-absorbed by forests and oceans may be over-optimistic.[7]

Indeed, in April 2008, James Hansen, head of NASA's Goddard Institute for Space Studies in New York, was calling for the EU target to be cut to 350 ppm, in the light of research suggesting that a level of 550 ppm, previously thought to result in 3 degrees of warming, would more likely mean a rise of 6 degrees Celsius in average global temperature. He commented: 'What we have found is that the target we have all been aiming for is a disaster – a guaranteed disaster.'[8]

The second problem is that a 2-degree or 3-degree rise in temperature, which sounds pleasant enough to those of us enjoying temperate climates, is already too much. We should not forget that this is an increase in global average temperature. In some parts of the world even a small rise is too much, and in fact it is likely to be rather more than 2 degrees in some vulnerable areas even if we do manage to stay below the 450 ppm mark.

What difference does it make?

Climate change is not simply a matter of temperatures rising. In that respect the term 'global warming' is misleading, because it's all to easy to think that if summer in the UK is chilly and wet, even to the extent of causing widespread floods, climate change can't be happening. But this in fact illustrates one of the most obvious effects of climate change, which is the increasing unpredictability of weather, even in a climate as typically unpredictable as our own. This can lead to extremes that previously have been rarely, if at all, experienced. And where a region is already prone to extremes of weather, such as drought or flooding, there is a risk that those extreme 'weather events' may be dangerously intensified, and may also become more frequent and less predictable.

Some examples

- The Indian state of Orissa is seeing new extremes of temperature. Between 1987 and 2001 the recorded maximum was 6.6 degrees higher than anything previously experienced, with a corresponding fall of 5 degrees in the lowest temperature.

- Across India as a whole, the average of 120 rainy days annually has fallen to 80. Before 1957 the percentage of years with normal (or above) rainfall ranged from 67 to 90 per cent. Since 1957 those percentages have fallen to 32 to 68 per cent.[9]

- In the Peruvian Andes, the ice-covered area was reduced by 22 per cent between 1970 and 1997. Mount Huascarán, Peru's most famous mountain, has lost 12.8 km^2 of ice, or 40 per cent of its ice area compared to 30 years ago.[10]

- In Rwanda in 1987, malaria incidence increased by 337 per cent. Four-fifths of that increase was put down to changes in rainfall and temperature.[11]

- In Kenya the melting of the glaciers on Mount Kenya provides the clearest evidence of climate change. The maximum temperature in Kericho, a highland area in

---

the Rift Valley province, where most of Kenya's tea exports are grown, has increased by 3.5 degrees Celsius in the past 20 years. The Kenya Meteorological Department has noted a very high variability in rainfall with severe drought becoming prevalent.[12]

Anyone working in international development, particularly in dealing with natural disasters, will have become increasingly aware of climate change in the past couple of decades. While most of the evidence is anecdotal, it is very clear that people living in vulnerable parts of the developing world have been only too conscious that things are not how they used to be. People in poor communities who know nothing of climate change and its causes readily offer their views about increasing extremes of weather. Typically they comment that the floods, droughts, hurricanes and so on that are, for them, an inevitable part of life are occurring more frequently and with greater intensity than in the relatively recent past.

Voices from El Salvador
- *Francisco Chávez, a prawn farmer in San Hilario, a rural area in El Salvador:* 'Hurricane Mitch [in 1998] caused houses to flood, especially in the low-lying areas. But the damage in Hurricane Stan [in 2005] was much worse than in previous hurricanes. We lost 80 per cent of our crops. It was very much worse than before. The

river where we had done prawn farming since 1996 burst its banks.'

- *Dominica Eschevarría, a fisherman's wife in San Luis la Herradura, El Salvador:* 'We definitely have more hurricanes and floods than we used to. I've lived here all my life and it wasn't like this before. Strong winds and big waves from the sea cause more floods now.'
- *Mauricio Henriquez, San Hilario:* 'Changes begin with deforestation in other parts of the world, like Brazil. Some years there's a lot of rain and other years there's drought. We also lose production because of our own deforestation.'

Christian Aid[13]

What will the future hold?

We all know from experience how difficult it is for weather forecasters to predict the weather, even over a very short period of time. Predicting how the climate will change is a considerable scientific challenge, and non-scientists can only wonder at the complexity of climate change modelling. Unsurprisingly, climate scientists are reluctant to commit themselves to detail and, as already indicated, predictions are constantly being revised, but there are nonetheless some general, and highly disturbing, conclusions to be drawn from their work.

The IPCC Fourth Assessment report predicts that the

average global temperature may rise by about 3 degrees Celsius by the end of the twenty-first century, while sea levels could rise by as much as 59 centimetres. The extreme weather events already exemplified are 'very likely' to become more frequent and more extreme. And the effects of changes such as these are going to be felt in every area of life, impacting in particular on the availability of food and water, on health, housing, economics and national security. In our global society, no one is going to be immune from such effects. And in addition we can expect to have to grapple with difficult ethical issues relating to biodiversity, population and migration.

The impact of global warming on health is particularly worrying. The countries most vulnerable to climate change are also for the most part those whose public health structures are unable to cope with its effects. And bodies such as the World Health Organisation have for some time been pushing for greater awareness on the part of health professionals as to what those effects are likely to be. Here are some examples:

- In Bangladesh: increased salinity in coastal areas will result in more cases of hypertension, premature birth (caused by pre-eclampsia), acute respiratory disease and skin diseases.
- In Nepal, rising temperatures and increased flooding, especially in the Kathmandu valley, are causing outbreaks

of typhoid, even in winter, along with more instances of vector- and water-borne diseases.

- In Zambia, severe flooding has already resulted in a fourfold increase in malaria, while prolonged drought is associated with a higher incidence of dysentery.
- Across Africa, a greater incidence of malaria, the world's biggest killer, is predicted: in Sudan malaria is ceasing to be seasonal but occurring all year round; Benin is seeing outbreaks of urban malaria, with children under five the main victims; and malaria-bearing mosquitoes are living longer (because of increased humidity) and are likely to be travelling further and to higher altitudes as temperatures rise.

UNFCCC 13th Conference of Parties[14]

Medical researchers are caught in a vicious circle. They admit the need for more research in order to establish correlations between climate and health. But this has to be balanced against the urgent need to take preventative action now, even though this will, if effective, reduce the evidence for a link to global warming.

Nonetheless, this is how it is, and how it will be, for some of the world's poorest people. In later chapters we will come back to the injustice of poor people being most affected by the carbon emissions of the rich. We will also look later at how it is possible to prevent an already bad situation from getting worse. But as far as the basic facts of climate change go, this is the first part of the message that the Church is called to proclaim. So how will we go about it?

The challenge of prophecy

In the opening verses of Revelation 1, the word 'revelation' or 'apocalypse' (1:1) is followed almost immediately (in 1:3) by John's reference to his book, the written form of his vision, as 'the prophecy'. So the implication[15] is that for John the two ideas are very closely related: making known what is unknown is a prophetic action, or at least a part of it. But John is doing more than recording a visionary experience in writing. His revelation, like prophecy, is designed to evoke a response: 'blessed are those who hear and who keep what is written in it' (1:3). Without that, prophecy itself fails, and the prophetic action is incomplete.

Speaking prophetically in the face of the climate crisis undoubtedly poses a challenge to the Church, which in recent years has tried hard to be accommodating rather than confrontational. When the Church does speak out, there is too often the uncomfortable feeling that it has failed either to accommodate or to challenge. Too often its leaders talk about things outside their experience; too often their solutions to the world's problems are platitudinous, and about as effective as a mobile phone without a signal.

There is a further complication within the Church itself,

which is that it is increasingly losing its community identity. In the UK this has been reflected in efforts to launch online churches, and to promote midweek services for commuters in cities rather than Sunday services in people's home towns and villages. While these initiatives may well create mini Christian communities, they do not result in an effective community voice, at least not at present, although there may well be potential for that in the future.

The first challenge, as already suggested, is to tell it like it is. And that means opening our eyes to the hard facts of climate change and being well informed and realistic about its effects. It means speaking honestly, showing people, as John does, 'what must soon take place'.

And the second challenge is to tell it in a way that provokes not just a response but an appropriate response, one that is proportionate to the immense size of the problem. This will be an underlying theme in the chapters that follow. But it is worth stating at the outset my conviction that recycling our rubbish is no way to save the planet. I have nothing at all against recycling; indeed I am very keen on it. But it is well within my comfort zone: it is easy to do and it makes me feel good for doing it. That, after all, is how we like things to be. Yet if we persuade ourselves that this is enough, then we have not even heard a prophetic message, let alone replied in a way that is remotely worthy of being seen as constituting an element in the whole action of prophecy.

Speaking together

Most of us probably think of prophecy, if we think about it at all, as an individual thing. Jeremiah and John the Baptist were typical prophets – loners, just them against the world as it was then constituted. And if we think about their message, it seems it is always doom-laden, a call to repent before it's too late. Little wonder, then, that we find the idea of a prophetic Church hard to deal with. Yet that is exactly what we are missing: a prophetic voice that is not a single voice, but many; a prophetic message that is not about individual sin but collective sin; and it is worth remembering that part of the climate change message has to do with the original meaning of 'repentance' – turning around, doing things differently.

Despite all our electronic communications and media opportunities that the biblical prophets could never have dreamt of, a lone voice is no way to address global warming. Even though Al Gore has had the resources and the stamina to maintain a one-man campaign that has been worldwide and extraordinarily effective, the dedication of one individual can never be an adequate response to a global crisis, nor should we allow it to be.

The great strength of the Christian Church lies in its numbers. It does not have to depend on the voice of one person – even if that person is a bishop or an archbishop – to convey its message and nor should it. If the leaders of the churches across the world could together speak out about climate change, their message would be hard to ignore. If they could combine their voices with those of the other world religions, their message would be impossible to ignore. There are reasons, of course, why that does not happen, not least the almost intractable problem of getting Christians to speak with a united voice on anything, and then to encourage others to join them. 'What must soon take place' will not wait until we've sorted out our disagreements or until we've learnt to stop trying to do our own thing. It needs a united voice of prophecy and it needs it now.

The idea that human activity affects the weather is one that has only quite recently been accepted. This is worth bearing in mind when people talk about the 'sin' of humankind in bringing this situation about. We weren't sinners, we just didn't know it was possible – although now that we do know, that changes everything. Al Gore, in his film *An Inconvenient Truth*, makes the point by quoting Mark Twain: 'What gets us into trouble is not what we don't know. It's what we know for sure that just ain't so.' But we do at least have a chance – a small window of opportunity – to put some of this right. If we shy away from that, if we choose to protect our current privileged lifestyles at the expense of both our fellow human beings and the world around us, then that truly is sinful.

Questions for discussion

1. How would you go about describing climate change and its effects to (a) a child, (b) your church, and (c) your MP? Would your overall message be any different? And if so, how and why?
2. What would it mean for you if the churches spoke with a truly prophetic voice? What would be your role?

Chapter 2

False Prophets

All he hath lieth in his tongue, and his religion is to make a
noise therewith.

> John Bunyan, *The Pilgrim's Progress*
> (Christian's assessment of Talkative)

What we believe about climate change is crucially important,
because our beliefs determine what, if anything, we are going
to do about it. So it is essential to address the question of
climate change denial early on in this debate, and examine
what people believe and why they believe it.

Most of us will not have the depth of technical knowledge
to work out the details of climate change for ourselves, nor
the implications of those scientific findings. So we rely on
other people for more than the science: we depend on them to
a large extent to guide our interpretation and, therefore, our
behaviour.

That is why it is so important to recognise and confront the
people I am calling 'false prophets'. If we don't understand
what is driving them, and their reasons, hidden or explicit, for
denying climate change, we will feel that we should at least
give them the benefit of the doubt. And all the time we're

having our civilised arguments and discussions, nothing gets done and the effects of climate change become increasingly hard to deal with.

The letters to the seven churches

The letters to the churches in Revelation 2 and 3 have much to say to the Church in the twenty-first century. That is true whether we look at each letter separately and study it in its original geographical context, or whether we take the view that the seven are to be read as one, addressed to the Christian churches as a whole. And the theme of false prophets is of obvious importance.

The emergence of people seeking to lead the faithful astray has always been closely associated with the approaching end of time. Jesus himself gave warning of it, as is recorded in the apocalyptic passages in the synoptic Gospels. In Mark's Gospel, for example, referring to 'those days', Jesus says, 'False messiahs and false prophets will appear and produce signs and omens, to lead astray, if possible, the elect' (Mark 13:22). There is a similar prediction in 2 Peter (probably written some 30 or 40 years later): 'There will be false teachers among you, who will secretly bring in destructive opinions ... because of those teachers the way of truth will be maligned' (2 Pet. 2:1–2).

We should not be tempted to dismiss false prophets as a

piece of apocalyptic extravagance. False teachers pose as big a threat to today's worldwide Church as they did to the fledgling Christian groups of the first century, as many have discovered to their cost. And it's worth remembering that the message to the church at Ephesus (Rev. 2:1–7) refers to false teaching at the highest level of Christian leadership and acknowledges the wisdom of the Ephesians in rejecting it: 'You have tested those who *claim to be apostles* but are not, and have found them to be false' (2:2). While the Greek word *apostolos* originally meant simply someone who is 'sent out', in Christian circles it was very quickly applied to the key figures in the early Church, probably comprising the eleven disciples and a few others such as Barnabas. This is the understanding of Paul, when he refers to himself as 'the least of the apostles', and John's use of the word has to be understood as having this restricted meaning. Interestingly, Paul himself has a similar warning about people he describes as 'boasters' – upstarts in the Christian community – who are 'false apostles, deceitful workers, disguising themselves as apostles of Christ' (2 Cor. 11:13). These are none other than the ministers of Satan, who 'disguise themselves as ministers of righteousness' (11:15).

The false apostles of climate change

Is it going too far to talk about climate change, and the people who deny it is happening, in such terms? If we genuinely believe that the climate crisis, if left unchecked, will eventually spell the end of human life, and much else, on our planet, then no language is too strong to condemn those who try to persuade us that nothing untoward is happening.

This chapter is about denial. Who is it who is saying that the climate is not changing, or if it is, it's only in accordance with natural processes? Who is it who is saying that yes, the climate is changing but there is nothing we can or should do about it? And why are they saying it? Then there are the more subtle forms of denial: choosing not to hear what is going on, not to react.

Voices from outside: denying the science

The early Church was not only under threat from individual false prophets coming from outside. There were threats from fringe groups as well, such as the Nicolaitans (Rev. 2:15), a short-lived heretical group whose teachings are unknown. Similarly, the voices denying climate change today are heard particularly clearly outside and on the fringes of the Church. As we shall see later, when their message is taken on and added to within the Church, we are dealing with a particularly powerful mix.

'The correct policy response to a non-problem is to have the courage to do nothing.' This is the philosophy of one of the UK's most colourful climate change deniers, Christopher

Monckton, sometime scientific adviser to Margaret Thatcher. 'Go home, there is nothing to worry about', was the message on one of Monckton's banners at the 13th Conference of Parties to the UN Framework Convention on Climate Change held in Bali in December 2007. It may be tempting to dismiss this as English eccentricity, and it is important to remember that none of Monckton's publications on climate change has been subject to peer review by other scientists. Yet the idea of having the courage to do nothing is a very appealing one, when the alternative seems to be such a threat to our comfortable lifestyles.

Monckton's main argument is that while global warming may be happening, greenhouse gas emissions are not responsible. Instead, rising temperatures are said to be the result of the sun going through an unprecedented level of activity, together with the earth's climate readjusting after unusually low temperatures at the end of the twentieth century.

The solar activity argument gained popular currency thanks to a now discredited UK TV documentary in 2007 called *The great global warming swindle*. Behind it was a theory developed by a Danish scientist, Henrik Svensmark, of the Danish National Space Center. His argument is that when solar wind (streams of electrically charged particles from the sun) is weak, fewer infra-red rays are deflected away from the earth. This creates more charged particles in the earth's atmosphere, inducing more clouds to form, so cooling the climate. Conversely, if the sun's output of rays is strong, there is less cloud cover and the planet warms up.

The Svensmark theory has been challenged by scientists at both Lancaster and Reading Universities, who have shown that cosmic rays make only a very weak contribution to cloud formation, with the Lancaster scientists concluding, somewhat reluctantly, that there has been no significant correlation between variations in solar activity and the cloudiness and temperature of the earth. This endorses, and indeed goes beyond, the IPCC view that 'since temperatures began rising rapidly in the 1970s, the contribution of humankind's greenhouse gas emissions has outweighed that of solar variability by a factor of about 13 to one.'[1]

Why this evangelical pursuit of a scientific lost cause? There is a clue in the position of one of Christopher Monckton's associates at Bali, Professor Emeritus William J. R. Alexander of the University of Pretoria. Africa, he said, requires 'trade not aid', and one aspect of trade he would like to see is the proliferation of coal-fired power stations, rather than renewable energy which he dismisses as ineffective.

Economics is often mentioned in the context of climate change denial. A former Chancellor of the Exchequer, Nigel Lawson, claims that the risks of greenhouse gas emissions are not as great as scientists suggest and that the costs of curbing such emissions are too great to contemplate.[2] Referring to global warming as a new religion, he is reported as saying: 'We appear to have entered a new age of unreason, which threatens to be as economically harmful as it is profoundly disquieting.' Yet in 2006 the so-called *Stern Review*, a UK Government report by Lord Stern of Brentford, argued that climate change did not mean opting out of economic growth and development.[3] Since then Lord Stern has suggested that his cost predictions were too low, given that climate change was happening faster than had previously been thought. Even so, there are great gains to be had for industry and technology, and denial of the facts of climate change for reasons to do with trade is an ostrich-like response.

Bishop James Jones, the Anglican Bishop of Liverpool, in the 2007 St George's lecture at Windsor, offered his own way, as a non-scientist, for answering climate change deniers, with four questions taken from George Monbiot:

If you reject the [IPCC] explanation for planetary warming, you should ask yourself the following questions:

1. Does the atmosphere contain carbon dioxide?
2. Does atmospheric carbon dioxide raise the average global temperature?
3. Will this influence be enhanced by the addition of more carbon dioxide?
4. Have human activities led to a net increase of carbon dioxide?

If you are able to answer 'no' to any one of them, you

should put yourself forward for a prize. You will have turned science on its head.[4]

So yet another form of denial – the one that says 'I'm not a scientist' – is confronted and challenged.

Making excuses: China and India

Denial is not confined to saying climate change is not happening or that if it is, it is not because of human activity. Denial covers all aspects of Monckton's mantra about 'the courage to do nothing'. And one of the most common forms of inaction, arguably more common than appeals to scientific truth, is to make excuses. These range from 'There's nothing I (little me) can do in the face of a global problem' to 'There's no point in us (the UK or even the EU) doing anything while America/China/India does nothing'.

This rather self-righteous argument simply seeks to preserve the status quo on the basis of information that is looking increasingly outdated. It is not the case that these countries are doing nothing, despite the attitude of the US Bush Administration (as opposed to many US state governments) and despite the rapid growth in carbon emissions by the two developing nations. There is also a refusal to recognise that the per capita emissions of both India and China are roughly half the per capita emissions of Europeans, the implication being that we don't see why other countries should reach the same level of development as us.

It is of course true that information about China, for example, is notoriously hard to come by. Yet, like India, this is a country that is particularly vulnerable to the effects of global warming: increased temperatures may dry up the rivers that provide water for the arid north while unusual rainfall patterns are causing increased flooding in the south. The air pollution that characterises the major cities has also received unwelcome publicity in the light of the 2008 Beijing Olympics.

A speech by the Chinese President, Hu Jintao, in advance of the July 2008 G8 summit in Hokkaido, Japan, made it clear that climate change measures are very much in the country's interest. President Hu emphasised five key groups of measures to combat climate change:

- controlling greenhouse gas emissions, including exploring new forms of industrialisation, energy saving, afforestation and developing a low-carbon economy;
- enhancing adaptation capacity, through conservation projects, environmental impact assessments, and improving the use of water resources;
- making use of innovations in science and technology, including accelerating research and development both nationally and internationally;
- setting up institutional mechanisms to address climate change, which means improving environmental laws and

regulations, building capacity on early warning systems and disaster risk reduction;

- raising awareness and encouraging public participation.[5]

Admittedly, this is mainly for the future, but it can no longer be said that China is 'doing nothing'. Indeed, there have already been small-scale environmental projects in rural China for some years, run by organisations such as the Amity Foundation, that are developing alternatives to fossil fuels.

The Amity Foundation
In Qinghai Province, the Amity Foundation, a Christian organisation, is installing biogas systems and greenhouses for farming families living at altitudes of 2500 metres or more. One beneficiary is Zhou Xianlong, a farmer from Chindu county. Mr Zhou and his family live 3840 meters above sea level and the winters are long and cold. Nonetheless, Mr Zhou, who has now built himself an additional greenhouse, is growing ten different kinds of vegetables, including tomatoes, celery and chilli peppers, which he is able to sell as well as provide food for his family. The biogas project converts animal waste into power and fertiliser and is sufficient to provide the family with heat, light and cooking facilities. As a result Mr Zhou no longer has to buy fuel (manure from yaks and cattle) or transport expensive vegetables from the provincial capital,

---

500 miles away. And his additional income enabled him to cope with unexpected expense during his wife's recent illness.

www.amityfoundation.org[6]

Voices from within: adding a religious dimension

It would be foolish to suggest that the voices challenging the science of climate change are all outside the Church. When I ask Christian audiences how many of them believe that climate change is not happening, it is roughly around 10 per cent who put their hands up. Some will quote science, a few will also quote the Bible, and the government conspiracy theory is never very far away either. An opinion poll commissioned for the *Observer* newspaper in June 2008 suggests that my unscientific head count is in fact an underestimate. According to the Ipsos Mori poll, the proportion of Britons who are unconcerned about climate change rose from 15 per cent to 23 per cent in the previous year, while most believe that it is partly due to natural causes, not just human activity. Similarly, say the pollsters, the majority of people in the UK believe that scientists are divided on the causes of climate change, and more than 20 per cent believe it has been blown out of proportion.

Within the Church, climate change denial can take on a very religious feel. The arguments put forward are not isolated instances. They reflect the clear and public teaching of some church leaders, revealing them to be not only misguided about climate change but weak in biblical and theological understanding as well. In these 'religious' arguments, the fact of climate change is not generally disputed, although its anthropogenic (human-induced) nature often is. Instead, the emphasis is on offering a non-scientific reason for climate change and the moral lessons we are to draw from that. In every case we are told that there is no action we can take to combat it. To try to resist is seen as undesirable (and unchristian), if not impossible. And while it may be the case that the views of the general public are influenced by which newspaper they read, and will fluctuate according to the whims of newspaper proprietors or individual journalists, Christian views are likely to be much more entrenched if there is perceived to be church backing for them.

God's punishment

You don't have to know much about the geography of south Asia to know that Bangladesh is one of the countries most at risk from climate change. The country is low lying, and much of its southern region is made up of the vast delta area formed by the mouths of the Ganges. Rising sea levels caused by warming temperatures and an influx of glacier melt from the Himalayas are leading to extensive erosion of the coastline, with thousands of people already homeless and moving further inland as a result. Like the island of Tuvalu, Bangladesh is slowly drowning.

The country is also vulnerable in other ways. Like its neighbours, it is naturally prone to cyclones and flooding, and climate change is causing those cyclones to happen more often and with greater intensity. Yet in the west the problem is not too much water but too little. Droughts in West Bengal are also increasing in severity thanks to the rising temperatures.

In November 2007 Bangladesh was struck by Cyclone Sidr and thousands of people died. I visited the area six months later and asked people about the cyclone which, they said, was much more severe than what they were used to. Why did they think it was so bad? The answer came with monotonous regularity: God was punishing them for their sins. There was, they said, little point in trying to construct more substantial houses and shelters, because God would punish them again. Rudimentary sheets of corrugated iron, the best that relief workers could offer them by way of repairs, were not going to keep God out.

Where did this conviction come from? Where did people get this mindset that is causing such inertia and a resignation that will surely have tragic consequences? The first thing to say is that 'God' here means both the Christian God and Allah: the same belief is widespread among Christians and Muslims alike. And the second thing is that the false teachers appear to be the local religious leaders. From a Dhaka mosque one Friday, the imam's voice rang out over the loudspeakers: 'Why is it so hot? Why is hell overflowing?

Because you are sinners.' Down in the delta area the local Christian priest told me how the cyclones were punishing marital infidelity in his village.

These false prophets, who maybe merit the biblical designation of false apostles, are dangerous because their teaching is stopping people from taking any measures to protect themselves and reduce the risk next time disaster strikes. Biblically and theologically, it is flawed teaching. Neither the God of the Bible nor the God of the Koran uses his good creation to punish people. The Christian clergy cite the plagues inflicted on the Egyptians (Exod. 8—9) in support of their argument, even though these events were not a punishment on God's own people and are most likely an example of the wisdom of hindsight, as the historians of the winning side recount their victories over their enemies.

It should be said that such views are not coming from the top of the Christian hierarchy, from the bishops. But the numerically tiny Christian Church in Bangladesh (well below 0.5 per cent of the population) should not be allowed to become divided by false teaching. And the consequences of inaction by Christians and Muslims alike in a country under extreme threat are far-reaching.

The end is near: US evangelicals divided
'God gave us these things to use. After the last tree is felled, Christ will come back.' Those were the words of James G. Watt, President Ronald Reagan's first Interior Secretary, to

the US Congress back in 1981, and they are not untypical of
the environmental thinking of the Christian right in America,
at least until very recently.

A number of factors are at work here. First and foremost,
there is an evangelical emphasis on the literal truth of Scripture. Genesis tells us that God gave human beings 'dominion'
over plant and animal life (Gen. 1:28–30), and this has been
interpreted to mean a divinely appointed right for humans to
use the earth as they will. A US millionaire, interviewed for a
UK TV programme called *God is Green*, broadcast in Feb-
ruary 2007, had made his fortune in mountain-top coal
mining. Yet for all the carbon emissions his activities caused,
he saw no need to change: God gave Adam dominion, so
nature is ours to control and exploit for our own benefit.
While others have taken the view that this so-called dominion
should be interpreted as caring for and sustaining creation,
the literalists have continued to take it at face value.

Closely associated with this is the view that the earth will
literally be destroyed in the last days (without any of the hope
for a new earth set out in Revelation 21) and that this time is
imminent. This line of thinking is not unrelated to the view
that conflict in the Holy Land is a sign of the approaching end
and therefore to be welcomed. So, the argument goes, there is
no point in worrying about environmental degradation.
Helping to destroy the earth may even be a virtue.

Then there are lingering prejudices about environmentalism that have been characteristic of evangelicalism

generally, not just in the States. The success of Christian environmentalism back in the 1980s was overshadowed by suspicion in some parts of the Church, with their activities being dubbed 'tree-hugging' at best and at worst 'pagan'. An important contributing factor to this stereotyping has been the traditional evangelical stress on personal salvation, which has no place for non-human creation. And a final compli-cating factor in the States has been an ideological one. Bishop James Jones speaks of an encounter with 'a leading and influential American evangelical' who 'sincerely believed that the response needed from God-fearing, flag-loving Americans was to be vigilant and sceptical about the scientific claims about climate change, to be protective of American business and jobs and to challenge the godless liberalism that under-mined traditional moral virtues especially in the area of family values.'[7] So protection of US interests, coupled with religious tradition, has built up into a powerful force within the country and within the Federal Government.

Attitudes seemed to be shifting among the Christian right, as people came to understand more about global warming and its likely impact. In October 2005, the National Asso-ciation of Evangelicals, which boasts a membership of some 30 million Americans, adopted a 'call to civic responsibility', that emphasised every Christian's duty to care for the planet and the role of government in safeguarding a sustainable environment. One of the key people behind this was the Revd Richard Cizik, who claims to have been 'converted' at a climate change conference in Oxford in 2002, thanks to the arguments of evangelical scientists, particularly Sir John Houghton.

Since 2005, however, there have been mixed messages coming from conservative evangelicals. Richard Cizik has been accused of promoting his personal opinions, and other evangelical leaders have argued that abortion, stem cell research and other moral issues are more important concerns for them. Climate change, they say, is being used simply to divert attention from these moral issues. The debate seems to have been complicated by the presence in the US environmental movement of population control activists. This group is not only hostile to Christianity but believes, or is assumed to believe, that the answer to climate change lies in reducing population numbers by abortion, sterilisation and so on.

Seeing climate change as a distraction from 'great moral issues' can only be regarded as a form of denial. Among some evangelical leaders certain religious and political interests have prevailed, with the result that a hugely influential movement is divided.

The American conservative evangelical movement has more than its fair share of false prophets. What they have in common is a belief that climate change need not, or should not, be resisted, and while this message is now weakened by internal divisions, it is still a powerful influence on church members, thanks to its endorsement by so many of their leaders.

God's in charge

Underlying all this is a view that God is in charge and there is nothing human beings should be doing to interfere with his purposes. This is the case whether climate change is seen as God's punishment or whether there is an understanding that God has put humankind in charge of creation to use it as we wish: if creation is destroyed in the process, that is part of God's plan.

Taking significant steps to combat global warming is in no sense to interfere with God's purposes. Quite the reverse. A thoughtful reading of the Bible and theological reflection will show us that care for creation and particularly for our fellow human beings is deeply rooted in Christian faith. We shall attempt to address the theological underpinning of climate change concerns in the chapters that follow. However, there is one further point to be made in relation to false prophets, or, more accurately, as a consequence of dealing with them.

The church at Ephesus: abandoning love

The church at Ephesus, addressed in Revelation 2, offers a salutary lesson. The Ephesian Christians are commended for their unflagging resistance to false prophets, but their religious fervour has resulted in something even more destructive than false teaching: a lack of love, the very foundation of their faith.

If scientific fact does not propel us into taking action against global warming, the love which we owe our fellow human beings, already suffering greatly from the effects of climate change, surely demands of us a Christian response of love. I have suggested already that our actions on climate change must be proportionate to the problem, taking account of its global dimensions, not just its local ones. Similarly, our response must also be compassionate, drawing us alongside the people of Kenya afflicted with drought, the people of Bangladesh made homeless by floods. Yet the voices that call on us to do all the right things, in terms of saving energy, cutting carbon and protecting biodiversity, often lack a compassionate tone. Like the church at Ephesus, today's Church, as it formulates its climate change message, needs to be sure that it is also responding to John's call to 'do the works you did at first' (Rev. 2:4), to recover its message of love, if it is to be truly prophetic.

Questions for discussion

1. Who are today's false prophets? How do they influence the voice of the Church?
2. How would you answer someone who argues that climate change is natural? How could your church support you in this debate?

Chapter 3

The Injustice of Climate Change

In a very broad and general way, we can talk about climate change as an issue that impels us to think about God's justice and how we are to echo it in our world.

Rowan Williams, Archbishop of Canterbury[1]

The church at Laodicea (Rev. 3:14–22): 'sluggish in serving God's justice'

Most preachers and public speakers will tell you that it's easier to engage with opposition, even hostility, than it is with indifference. Opposition may be challenging and difficult, but there is at least a point of contact, a starting point for conversation. When people are neither openly for you nor against you, but merely indifferent, there is nothing.

This is the picture of the church at Laodicea, the only church addressed in Revelation 2 and 3 where there is nothing good to be said for it. Laodicea was a wealthy city and its church members were drawn from an affluent society. And their spiritual lives seem to have been characterised by smug contentment. Like their water supply, drawn from a hot spring but cooled down by the time it reached the city, the Laodiceans were lukewarm.

The medieval mystic Hildegard of Bingen draws heavily on the Book of Revelation in her own visionary writings. And she sees the Laodiceans reflected in Christians who are reluctant to proclaim their faith; she says they are 'lukewarm and sluggish in serving God's justice'.[2]

Within the Church today, this sluggishness, or indifference, typically takes the form of a take-it-or-leave-it attitude to faith. If we are modern-day Laodiceans, we are content to let other people preach the Gospel, because evangelism is not really our thing, although we broadly agree with what they say. A church made up entirely of such people can never grow – it will simply die away, as did Laodicea.

Outside the Church there is plenty of lukewarmness as well, although the ultimate victims are not the self-satisfied ones themselves, because being indifferent means shutting your eyes to what you don't want to see. It means being deliberately unaware – not wanting to know what's going on around you. Being sluggish in matters of justice is to fail to see or understand that there is any injustice to be addressed.

Justice and climate change

It should already be clear from what has been said in the two previous chapters that many of the countries most vulnerable to global warming are also among the world's poorest countries. And this is borne out by IPCC scientists.

The IPCC has highlighted the four areas of the world that it considers most vulnerable to climate change. These are *small island developing states* (for example, the disappearing island of Tuvalu but also the West Indies, Cuba, Cyprus and Malta), *Africa* (which contains no fewer than 33 of the world's 49 so-called least developed countries), *mega-deltas* (especially in Asia, for example Bangladesh) and the *polar regions*. Africa, they say, is one of the most vulnerable continents to climate variability and change 'because of multiple stresses and low adaptive capacity'. What this basically means is that the continent's low level of development restricts its ability to adapt to changing conditions, with the possible exception of South Africa and excluding the North African States.

Quite apart from the geographic vulnerability of so many of the least developed countries, and therefore the likelihood of the poorest people in the world suffering most as a result of climate change, it is obvious that in any disaster, whether climate change-related or not, the poor are hit hardest. We saw this to be true after Hurricane Katrina in New Orleans in August 2005. Even in the world's most highly developed nation, it was the poorer people who had difficulty escaping the devastation, and many have not yet returned from temporary accommodation far from where they want to be. After the Asian tsunami the previous year (clearly not climate-related but a disaster on a huge scale), it was the rich who had the education and the money to rebuild their lives. The poor fishermen of Tamil Nadu, the worst-affected Indian state, were still homeless a year later while the state government debated where their homes should be rebuilt (which again was not where, as fishermen, they needed to be). Since then, the cyclones that have hit first Bangladesh and then Burma have taken their toll of poor families whose flimsy homes could not protect them, and left them prey to disease and malnutrition.

The many faces of injustice

It has become something of a cliché to say that climate change has most impact on those who have done least to cause it. In terms of carbon emissions, this is undeniably true. The rich countries of Western Europe have been calculated to be responsible for emitting around 12 metric tonnes of carbon per person per year, while in the United States the figure is nearer 24 metric tonnes. But for people in, say, Zambia, the figure is only 0.1 metric tonnes.[3] Since Zambia is likely to suffer more extreme climate events than, say, the United Kingdom, and since its poor communities have little or no resources to deal with them, this is clearly unfair – an injustice. However, like many clichés, the statement is also an over-simplification.

To start with, it tends to be developing countries that are responsible for damage caused by deforestation. This doesn't let the rich countries off the hook, of course, but it does make the justice argument rather more complex without invalidating it. If we look closely at the reasons for loss of trees, there is generally a poverty connection. All too often poor people have no alternative but to cut down trees for firewood. Deforestation has also been a characteristic of civil war in countries such as Sudan and Burundi, when combatants destroy woods and forests in order to flush out the enemy. In both cases, environmental damage is down to a way of life that poor people are virtually powerless to change.

Poor people are also powerless to resist what Friends of the Earth have called the 'land grab' for biofuel production. While objections to extensive biofuel production have focused largely on the rise in food prices caused by the loss of agricultural crops, the damage done to indigenous communities who are moved off their land receives much less publicity.

My personal view is that we should not be using an argument about injustice in order to point the finger of blame at the rich. Rather, we should acknowledge that there is a clear injustice in the inability of poor individuals, communities and nations to protect themselves against climate change, by comparison with the resources of richer people, communities and countries both to protect themselves and to continue with their own environmentally damaging lifestyle. We are in the business of restorative, not retributive, justice.

There are other injustices as well. One is the injustice done to future generations. It is our children and grandchildren who will have to live with the consequences of the damaging lifestyles of today's parents. For poor people and their children it will be worse. Most deaths from malaria in the developing world are those of children under the age of five. As rising temperatures cause malaria to spread, the disease will kill more and more children whose parents cannot afford medication or mosquito nets for them.

We need also to ensure that measures to combat climate change or to adapt to its effects do not themselves create injustices. The ongoing biofuels debate mentioned above is a case in point. In some cases the opportunity to grow industrial crops for fuel may be a welcome new source of income for poor farmers as part of a sustainable, mixed-crop approach, particularly when this helps to meet local energy needs and protects soil quality. But in other cases, crops grown for food have been destroyed and agricultural land has been given over to industrial crops, with devastating results for poor people whose lives and livelihoods depend on their produce.

Fuelling our carbon habit – with biofuels

How important is life and how important are cars? Life first, cars second.

Evo Morales, President of Bolivia[4]

The 200 kg of industrial maize needed to create fuel for just one 50-litre car tank of biofuel would, as agricultural maize, feed one person for a whole year.

Jean Zigler[5]

Over the past decade, in both South and North America, the production of industrial maize in place of the food crop has soared. Ethanol is blended into more than 50 per cent of the petrol sold in the United States, and production has risen from 1,300 million gallons in 1997 to an estimated 6,500 million gallons in 2007.

The US Secretary of Agriculture Ed Schafer has defended the use of ethanol, on the grounds that its production contributed 'only' 2 to 3 per cent of food price rises, although the IMF has suggested that the demand for biofuels is responsible for 70 per cent of the increase in corn prices.

In Latin America and the Caribbean commercial biofuel plantations are pushing small-scale and subsistence farmers off their land and monopolising water supplies, so squeezing out domestic food production.

Christian Aid[6]

To add insult to injury on the subject of biofuels, scientists are now suggesting that ethanol from maize does not in fact produce very significant carbon savings. So poor farmers are having to surrender their livelihoods not so that the planet can be saved but rather so that the North will be able to continue its gas-guzzling habit as the oil wells run dry.

Finally, the enthusiasm of some for a greener lifestyle has created an environmental movement that is undeniably middle class. We are already making it very hard for low-income families in the UK to adopt an environmentally friendly lifestyle: insulation, solar power and hybrid cars are all prohibitively expensive. And when legislation requiring such things is introduced, as inevitably it will be, we should not forget that lower-wage earners will find it hardest to comply. People in any country rarely drive polluting old bangers out of choice: it is because that is all they can afford. And telling people to choose a more expensive public-transport option is a non-starter.

Should we add in here the various forms of injustice that some might consider are being inflicted on the natural world? Is it possible to speak of justice in respect of animals and landscapes? This is a question for Chapter 4. However, I would suggest that while it is possible to understand what is meant by a statement like 'Melting ice flows, due to carbon emissions, is unfair on polar bears', this is not a moral assertion. This does not mean that the natural world cannot be included in theological reflection on climate change, but it does indicate that human suffering is of a different moral order from that of plants and animals.

What are Christians to conclude from all this? I suggest, quite simply, this. When we go to the real heart of the climate change debate, we should not expect to find there an academic question about scientific accuracy or even the environmental one about biodiversity. Instead, we find a deeply moral issue: that of injustice. It is this that a theological approach to climate change must also have at its centre; it is injustice in all its forms that the prophetic voice of the Church must address; and it is the victims of those injustices whom Christians are called to hold in their hearts.

Love and justice

The defining characteristic of Christianity is love. Christians believe in a God who loves us, and whose love for humankind has been ultimately revealed in the life, death and resurrection of his Son Jesus Christ. In the unloving climate of the ancient world, the love of Christians was sufficiently distinctive to be remarked on by those outside their faith. 'See how they love one another and how they are ready to die for each other', commented the third-century pagan writer Tertullian, who subsequently became a Christian himself. Jesus' new commandment to his followers, 'Love one another as I have loved you' (John 15:12), is echoed in the exhortations of Paul (especially in 1 Corinthians 13) and in the first epistle of John: 'Let us love, not in word or speech, but in truth and action'

(1 John 3:18). And since then Christians – and the churches – have endeavoured to behave accordingly, inevitably falling short along the way.

The concept of justice is closely bound up with love, and the Old Testament reveals both love and justice to be in the nature of God himself. The song of Moses in Deuteronomy 32 celebrates God in these terms: 'The Rock, his work is perfect, and all his ways are just. A faithful God, without deceit, just and upright is he' (v. 4). The song goes on to portray God as a loving parent:

> He sustained [Jacob] in a desert land,
> in a howling wilderness waste;
> he shielded him, cared for him,
> guarded him as the apple of his eye.
> As an eagle stirs up its nest,
> and hovers over its young;
> as it spreads its wings, takes them up,
> and bears them aloft on its pinions,
> the Lord alone guided him.
>
> Deuteronomy 32:10–12

In the New Testament, the Sermon on the Mount promises new life for the poor, the hungry and the victims of injustice (Matt. 5:2–12; Luke 6:20ff). Indeed, this central concern for love and justice is encapsulated in the mission of Jesus, who quoted Isaiah in the Nazareth synagogue and applied that prophecy to himself:

> The Spirit of the Lord is upon me, because he has anointed me to bring good news to the poor. He has sent me to proclaim release to the captives and recovery of sight to the blind, to let the oppressed go free, to proclaim the year of the Lord's favour.
>
> Luke 4:18–19

The love and justice that is shown us by God has to be reflected, even if inadequately, in our relationships with one another. This suggests that relational theology might be a helpful way forward in considering the effects of global warming.

Karl Barth's covenant theology

A few years ago I took a small group of bishops and other church leaders to Zambia and South Africa, to see the devastating effects of the HIV/AIDS epidemic in those countries. In the course of our many conversations we reflected together on what might be the best theological framework for discussing this difficult situation. Models that reflected a God who punishes – an idea much in vogue among some Christians at the time – were clearly inappropriate, as were models that promised physical healing in return for repentance.

It was David Atkinson, currently Bishop of Thetford, who suggested that the relational theology of Karl Barth might be a fruitful line of approach.[7] Barth's monumental work *Church Dogmatics* examines the eternally faithful and loving (covenant) relationship between God and humankind, whatever may befall them. This is, by implication, a model for human beings' relationships with one another. He also has much to say about the nature of the Christian community, which is crucial in our response to such difficult issues as HIV and climate change. It is a theological framework that is able to accommodate searching questions and new realities, and one that above all offers hope for the future.

Covenant and creation

In summary, Barth takes the concept of covenant relationships between God and human beings, familiar to us from the historical books of the Old Testament, and suggests that such a relationship existed from the very moment of creation. To take just one example, in 2 Samuel 7 we have God's covenant with King David, in the form of a promise to the King's successor: 'I will be a father to him, and he shall be a son to me. When he commits iniquity, I will punish him with a rod such as mortals use, with blows inflicted by human beings. But I will not take my steadfast love from him' (vv. 14–15). This is the ideal parent–child relationship that Barth sees as existing for all time. (For present purposes it is worth bearing in mind as well that this relationship rules out the punishment of human beings by the forces of nature.)

So covenant and creation are inextricably linked, and this finds fresh expression in the incarnation. In Barth's words, 'The purpose and therefore the meaning of creation is to make possible the history of God's covenant with man which has its beginning, its centre and its culmination in Jesus Christ.'[8]

So there is a oneness, an interconnectedness, between people, creation and God that has been present since human history began. This oneness reflects the three persons of the Trinity – Father, Son and Holy Spirit – who, Barth argues, are all present at creation and take part in the act of creation.

And it is surely in this context of interconnected relationships that we are to view human sinfulness. For sin lies in the breakdown of human relationships, revealed in the unjust distribution of resources which creates a chasm between rich and poor. Sin also lies in the loss of connectedness between human beings and the environment, which has brought about the crisis of global warming. And in all this there is, too, the breakdown of our own relationship with God.

The 'life of the children of God'

These theoretical relationships have, for Barth, a very practical outworking in the Christian community. His argument, very much in line with the exhortation in 1 John to 'love in truth and action', is that people who receive God's word are compelled to act in accordance with it. So we have both an inner life (our 'being') and an outward one, which is about 'doing', being in fellowship with others.

The command to love our neighbour as ourselves takes pride of place here. To obey it is nothing less than to praise God, and it is also central to Christian unity. The truth of this is evident if we think of examples where our unity has been broken: a lack of love will always be in there somewhere.

So the interconnectedness of the created order compels us to act out of love when part of that order is under threat or when a connection is broken. Such actions may be little different from anything done by people outside the community; the difference lies in the fact that for Christians there is no choice but to act – and to act in a way that is compassionate, wise and effective.

'Interconnectedness' – beyond the jargon

'Interconnectedness' is something of a cliché in environmental circles, used most frequently to emphasise human dependency on our planet and our duty of care (or 'stewardship'). In a Christian context, though, it has to assume a wider meaning. Our belief in a creator God demands that we recognise both nature's dependency on God and our own dependency on him; our concern for the natural world requires us to examine our place in it; and our love of justice, which we derive from the nature of God himself, has to flow through our human connections with one another.

We may choose to see in all this a network of interconnected relationships. And it is worth emphasising that this is a network rather than a hierarchy, even though the elements of the network do not necessarily enjoy the same status. This contrasts with the order that some see in the Book of Genesis, where humankind takes its place *below* God but *above* the plants and animals over which it exercises 'dominion' (Gen. 1:28). In the network of creation, the activities of one group of humans impact on another group and/or on the natural environment and vice versa. For example, warming of the ocean has an adverse impact on fish stocks, which in turn affects human food supply and leads to tensions and conflicts between human beings, whose activities have caused the warming in the first place.

Human networks: the case of the Inuit

The effect of climate change on indigenous peoples is being increasingly documented, as global warming impacts on their traditional lifestyle and livelihoods, and we will come back to this in Chapter 4. In December 2005 a group of Inuit from Canada and the United States filed a petition with the inter-American Commission of Human Rights alleging that the failure of the United States to reduce its greenhouse gas emissions was violating their human rights. So an international tribunal was confronted with the serious consequences of global warming for human health and culture. It also linked up the suffering of particular people in climate-sensitive territories with the actions of polluters elsewhere. Framing these issues in the language of human rights litigation effectively underlines the injustices that one group of people are inflicting on others.[9]

Gender injustice

It is not only the case that climate change has a disproportionate effect on poor people: it also disproportionately affects women. Women make up 70 per cent of the world's poor and have less access to financial resources, land, education and health-care than men. They are therefore less able to cope with the impact of climate change and less able to adapt.[10] It is also true that women and men have different perceptions of climate change and different degrees of dependency on the natural environment.

Women for Climate Justice, a network based in Berlin, has pointed out that women's participation in decision-making on climate policy is very low and therefore women's practical and strategic needs are not being properly taken into account. They say:

The participation of women ... is crucial for developing just, effective and efficient measures of climate protection. Climate protection needs women's expertise, their perspectives, their political support, and their engagement as key agents of change. It is important to recognise the diversity of women ... one 'token' woman at the table won't do it.[11]

Women's voices

It's the women who do the agricultural work and who have to prevent erosion. The women suffer first when the environment is destroyed: there's no water and they have to spend a long time going to get it. There are food shortages and if there is erosion homes get damaged. So they need to be trained to take proper care of nature, for the sake of the women of tomorrow. When there was a famine the men would sell off bits of the home including the windows and the roof. Then when there was nothing left they would go off to Tanzania and say they were refugees.

Madame Pélagie Simbinuba[12]

Women in Nepal are adamant about the need for training to allow them to increase their income through alternative livelihoods, such as goat rearing and poultry farming, following the loss of their monsoon crops to flooding:

We are far behind in terms of acquiring new skills. I think we also need information, training and seeing other alternatives. We want to know how women in other villages are managing their livelihoods.

Muna Mukeri[13]

Who is my neighbour? The message of the Gospels

Paul's famous statement of inclusiveness in Galatians 3:28 is a pretty good answer to the lawyer's question, 'Who is my neighbour?': 'There is no longer Jew or Greek, there is no longer slave or free, there is no longer male and female: for all of you are one in Christ Jesus.' This is one aspect of Barth's 'life of the children of God' – to live alongside each other without discrimination or differentiation. But there is more to it than this ideal, which is, after all, shared by very many non-Christians as well. The theology of John's Gospel shows us the extraordinary oneness of God the Father and the Son, a oneness which Christian believers are invited to share: 'As you, Father, are in me and I am in you, may they also be in us', prays Jesus (John 17:21). This is a relationship which unites us with one another and with God and which Paul frequently refers to when he talks about being 'in Christ'.

Given our oneness with God and with one another, it goes without saying that part of loving our neighbour means loving our fellow Christians as ourselves – something we seem to find extraordinarily difficult. But our neighbour is also our neighbour in our local, national and international human community, not just someone who shares our faith, as the parable of the Good Samaritan makes very clear. Global warming is the sign of the harm we are inflicting on people who are part of the body of Christ and on those who are not.

These are our neighbours – something we must never forget as we seek to halt the damage we are doing. If we do forget them, if we focus on making easy adjustments to our comfortable lives and averting our eyes from the bigger picture, then we are as guilty as the Laodicean church of the accusation of being lukewarm.

The very intimate nature of that neighbourliness is also an ideal we should not lose sight of. Will we be able to put our hands on our hearts and say yes, the efforts we have put into combating climate change are a true reflection of the God of love described in Deuteronomy: 'in a howling wilderness waste ... he shielded him, cared for him, guarded him as the apple of his eye' (Deut. 32:10)? If not, why not?

Questions for discussion

1. Who do you genuinely believe to be your neighbour?
2. What understanding of 'justice' do we need to develop if we are to show love to that neighbour?

Chapter 4

The Right to Live

Everyone has the right to a standard of living adequate for the
health and well-being of himself and of his family, including
food.

Article 25, Universal Declaration of
Human Rights (1948)

The Pergamum problem (Rev. 2:12–17)

Pergamum was the seat of government of the Roman province of Asia. What John calls 'Satan's throne' is likely to be a
reference to the imperial temple built there in 29 BC. So perhaps more than the other churches addressed, Christians in
Pergamum were conscious of what we would nowadays call
inter-faith relations. They needed to develop a way of
peaceful co-existence with the Roman regime and its religion,
having already witnessed the martyrdom of Antipas.

Their problem was that they had chosen a path of excessive
tolerance, apparently accepting those who ate food sacrificed
to idols and who engaged in immoral practices. Faced with
difficult choices, the church at Pergamum had chosen to skirt

round them, either out of a desire for fairness or in the hope of a quiet life.

The hard choices of climate change present a similar challenge. Most people are reluctant to opt for a course of action that represents increased financial cost or personal inconvenience, whether we're talking about energy, travel, food or something else, whether in our working lives or family lives. I have lost count of the times I have suggested to national and international church networks that they should cut out travel and conduct their meetings via telecommunications links, only to be told, 'It's not the same.' Well of course it isn't, but the planet won't be the same either unless we face up to these hard choices very soon.

The moral issues that confront us in the light of a changing climate are many and varied, and some of them will come to the fore in this chapter and the next. It is essential to remember that this is not a theoretical discussion, not an academic seminar on ethics. The choices we now have to make have the power to save lives or destroy them. So we need to begin by confronting the most basic of issues: how can we safeguard people's lives, their health and their food, as global warming threatens to undo much of what human progress has achieved in these areas in recent years?

Human rights

Thanks to a growing number of court cases where claimants have alleged infringement of their human rights to justify sometimes very trivial (not to say absurd) complaints, the whole concept of rights has become somewhat tarnished in the popular imagination. In the UK, legislation in 2007 that banned smoking in public places led to a number of cases alleging infringement of various human rights. It was argued that the right to enjoy one's own property and possessions was infringed when a taxi driver couldn't smoke in his own cab (if he had no passengers at the time) and that respect for their private and family life was infringed when patients in high-security hospitals (their home) were barred from smoking. Whatever one may think of such complaints – and smokers and non-smokers will most probably have very different views – the underlying rights to home and family life remain crucially important in a civilised society, and we shouldn't allow fundamental rights and freedoms to appear to be undermined or weakened by lawyers and litigants.

In addition, some Christians are deeply distrustful of the concept of human rights, seeing an unchristian liberalism in the exercise of certain human freedoms. Yet I believe that there is much we can learn from setting the rights movement in a Christian context. I am not discarding the relational theology outlined in the last chapter. Rather, I am using rights-based norms of ethical behaviour as a way to help us in preserving some of those crucial relationships from injustice and to deepen our relationship with God.

God and rights

The Bible does not speak the language of human rights, at least not overtly. We will look in vain for explicit references to human dignity, even to that most basic of human rights, the right to life. The basic commandment not to kill barely touches on the intricacies of all that is enshrined in the right to life. Even the command to love our neighbour as ourselves arouses in us a desire to limit the command, to restrict our behaviour, by asking the question, 'Who is my neighbour?' Yet the secular formulation of human rights, the very language of rights, is rooted in Christian belief.

Human beings derive their worth, their dignity, from being made in the image of God. For the German theologian Jürgen Moltmann this 'image' creates a two-way relationship. He writes:

Image of God means the full community of God ... Human rights mirror the right of the coming God and the future of humanity. The destiny of the human being to be the image of God indicates the indivisible right of God to the human being and, therefore, the irreducible dignity of the human being.[1]

In other words, as we have seen from relational theology, the image of God in us is indicative of God's concern for our well-being, and the image of God in others compels us to seek their well-being in addition to our own. This duty is enshrined within the Christian community and in the Church:

> In the name of the creation of the human being in the image of God ... the church is charged with responsibility for the humanity of persons as well as for their rights and duties in time.[2]

Moltmann also links the image of God reflected in human beings with our care for the natural world. He argues that if human beings have a right to the earth because they are made in God's image, then everyone has a right to a fair share of the earth's goodness. He condemns the 'plundering, exploitation, and the destruction of nature' that contradict human beings' right and dignity. He continues:

> The concentration of the basic necessities of life and the means of production in the hands of a few should be seen as a distortion and perversion of the image of God in human beings. It is unworthy of human beings and contradicts God's claim upon them.[3]

So being made in God's image entails not only rights but responsibilities: the responsibility to uphold the dignity of our fellow human beings; and the responsibility to maintain an equitable relationship with them and with the earth on which we depend. To fail in either of those responsibilities is to deface the image of God. So what particular rights and responsibilities are we talking about in the context of climate change?

Climate change and human rights

It is, I think, important to draw away from legal language at this point. While there may in the future be cases brought to court, enforcement of people's rights in the context of climate change is fraught with difficulty. Even more problematic is deciding who is responsible for each damaging act, particularly when the perpetrators may be based thousands of miles away. Nevertheless, we should not forget that these are natural rights that, in Europe at least, are enshrined in our national legal systems. It is, after all, a condition of countries wanting to join the European Union that they transpose the European Convention on Human Rights into national law, which is some indication of the importance placed upon fundamental rights and freedoms by secular governments.

There are various basic freedoms that are under threat from climate change: these have to include rights to food and health; in the case of people threatened by the disappearance of land as well as by extreme weather events, there is their right to a home (which will be bound up with the rights of migrants, an issue that will be addressed in Chapter 6); and, in the case of people living in the developing world, there is the right to continue to develop. And to put it very bluntly, if we do nothing ourselves to combat the effects of climate change, then we are guilty of infringing, morally if not legally, all these natural rights belonging to millions of people. To avoid incurring that moral responsibility, we have some hard choices to make.

Life and health

The consequences of climate change for the health of the world's poorest countries are potentially very serious indeed, not helped by the fact that the countries worst affected are also those with the weakest health infrastructures. There are also ethical dimensions similar to those outlined in the previous chapter. For example, there is a generational injustice: future generations will be affected more as temperatures rise, and children are always more at risk than adults. The World Health Organisation has estimated that 88 per cent of people affected by disease attributable to climate change are children under the age of five. And, as already indicated, the range of health consequences is considerable, including heat stress, allergies resulting from air pollution, vector-borne diseases (malaria, dengue fever), water-borne diseases, ill health resulting from a lack of food or water, and mental health problems.

One speaker at the UNFCCC Bali conference posed the ethical problem like this. The key reason for banning smoking was the harm that passive smoking causes to other people. Shouldn't we now consider climate change in the same way and address the damage that our carbon habit is inflicting on others? Banning carbon emissions in public places would certainly be a radical way forward, although it would still leave public health systems in the developing world in need of urgent improvement and investment, simply to deal with the health problems that have already emerged.

It almost goes without saying that animals suffer from climate change-related disease as well as humans, the knock-on effect being increased human suffering.

A cattle breeder in Senegal

In Senegal, climate change has added to problems associated with the decline in government services following independence in 1960. Gallo Samba Ba explains:

> In the past, the government was responsible for looking after the water infrastructures, the boreholes, the wells and the cattle troughs. Since independence local people have had to raise their own money to purchase or repair the material. The state withdrew completely.

Because of climate change there are more diseases today than in the past. Before, the forest was dense and the cattle would get lots of vitamins from the leaves of the trees. There was plenty of grass so the cows didn't have to walk such long distances to find straw and they didn't congregate in the same areas. Now, because of a large concentration of cattle in the areas where grass remains, when a cow or goat falls sick they can easily contaminate the rest of the cattle. And until 1960 the Senegalese government paid for vaccinations. Now we have to find the doctor and the money to find a cure and to vaccinate our cattle.

Christian Aid[4]

Life and food: the eucharistic community

Jesus said: 'I have compassion for the crowd, because they have been with me now for three days and have nothing to eat.'

Mark 8:2

Providing and sharing food is a significant characteristic of the Gospel story. Jesus begins his ministry by providing wine for the wedding at Cana; and his final hours are marked by a community meal with his disciples, a meal even richer in symbolism than the miracle at Cana yet one that still fulfils a basic human need and a key ritual obligation. In between there are glimpses of Jesus sharing food with all kinds of people, though more with those on the margins of society than with the rich. And food is frequently the subject of miraculous provision, from unexpected hauls of fish to the feeding of large crowds. Significantly too, Jesus himself often takes the initiative: after the resurrection he invites the disciples to take breakfast with him – a sign of his physical reality; while the miracle of the feeding of the four thousand comes about because of Jesus' compassion, his spontaneous recognition that the people around him need food.

Throughout the Bible there is a concern that no one should be without food and water. The hungry must be fed. Not to do so is to behave in a way that is 'unrighteous', unacceptable in the kingdom of God, as Jesus himself makes clear: 'Just as you did not do it to one of the least of these, you did not do it to me' (Matt. 25:45). There is too an acute awareness of the injustice that some should have too much food and others too little, memorably expressed in the song of Mary with its vision of a new order: 'he has filled the hungry with good things, and sent the rich away empty' (Luke 2:53).

It is therefore self-evident that the very real danger of millions more people being without food and the climate injustice that is bringing this about should weigh heavily on Christian communities in the twenty-first century. It is estimated that 854 million people already do not get enough to eat every day, and every year more than 6 million children under 5 die from hunger-related illness.[5] Climate change will make this situation worse. Some reports suggest that Africa's crop yields will be reduced by 10 per cent, and in some regions by much more.[6] In Tanzania, maize production is forecast to fall by 33 per cent. Climate change is likely to make areas that are already prone to drought drier still, with the Horn of Africa, Zimbabwe, Malawi and Zambia cited by the UN Food and Agriculture Organisation's Climate Change Group as the parts of Africa most at risk.[7]

Jesus' compassion for the crowd and his subsequent feeding miracle is much more than a fine gesture in unusual circumstances. Rather, it leads us to probe the deepest meaning of human beings producing and sharing food and our dependence on the natural world.

'The need to eat and drink', writes the Jesuit theologian Gustave Martelet, 'is common to the whole of mankind; but what is more, it is a need which the individual cannot meet satisfactorily except in *association* with others.'[8] Sharing food is the basis for personal, family and community relations. And for Christians there is a shared meal at the heart of their relationship with God and with one another – the Eucharist. Yet the symbolism of this meal is not to be treated as taking its meaning solely from the spiritual actions and beliefs of those participating in it. The bread and the wine are the fruit of human interaction with nature and human creative processes, and they are offered to rich and poor alike. Martelet continues: 'As the bread and wine bring to the table the symbolic loading of the world's culture, so we must accept that they evoke, too, the world's distress.'[9]

In other words, at the heart of our Christian lives as a community of faith, there is not only a reminder that rich and poor are united in the sacrament but also an implied imperative to ensure that the inequity between us is removed. When we set this alongside Barth's view[10] that the Christian community is defined by its willingness to act out of love for one's neighbour, we have a potent mix.

Food security: the hard questions

Early in 1976 the International Covenant on Economic, Social and Cultural Rights (ICESCR) came into effect. This included an Article which developed Article 25 of the UDHR quoted at the start of this chapter. Basically, Article 11 of the ICESCR sets out the implications of, first, the right to adequate food, and second, the right to be free from hunger, where it notes in particular the need to 'ensure an equitable distribution of world food supplies in relation to need'. Bearing in mind Gandhi's warning that there is enough in the world for everyone's need but not enough for everyone's greed, how are Christians to observe the human rights of others at a time when climate change is simply increasing the divide between rich and poor at the most basic level of human survival?

The absurdity of a world where obesity in the rich nations is rapidly leading to an unparalleled health crisis, while countless people in the poorest nations face a daily struggle to avoid starvation, almost beggars belief. It is a deeply immoral situation we cannot shrug off with trite comments about the poor being always with us, if only because the climate change crisis caused by the rich North and, what is almost worse, our responses to it seem to be causing the food crisis to spiral out of control. Something has to give, as a matter of urgency, and that necessarily will affect those of us who enjoy the luxury of comfortable living and cheap food.

The first thing we need to face up to is that our eating habits are making a substantial contribution to global warming. I have always been somewhat sceptical about the idea that the creation stories in Genesis demand that we become vegetarian. But the more I think about it, the more it seems to me that vegetarianism, or at least some moderation of our meat-eating habits, is an important element in maintaining the delicate balance of our planet.

A 2007 report by Compassion in World Farming, entitled *Global warning: climate change and farm animal welfare*,[11] sets out some stark figures. Citing statistics from the UN Food and Agriculture Organisation (the FAO), they say that total emissions from animal production – mainly methane and, to a lesser extent, carbon dioxide – amount to 18 per cent of human-induced emissions globally (while all forms of transport account for 14 per cent). The problem is exacerbated by the environmental impact of the use of land for pasture and for animal feed, including the degradation of pastures, water pollution and deforestation. Yet the FAO predict that by 2050 global meat and milk consumption will be double that of 2001, with the number of animals used rising from nearly 60 billion to 120 billion. 'Such a marked upsurge', comments the report, 'would have an overwhelming impact on climate change and the environment.'

Clearly there would be considerable advantage to human health in the North, not to mention the reduction in unacceptable factory farming processes that most animal-lovers would hope to see, if our concern for global warming could make us change our eating habits. But would that be at the expense of agriculturalists in the global South whose livelihoods may depend on the export of soya for animal feed?

Questions such as this pop up all over the place once we start to look into the consequences of the choices that face us in trying to reduce the impact of climate change. But the ethical response is straightforward. Our insatiable desire for meat, once seen as a luxury but now regarded as an everyday necessity, is having a devastating effect on the world's poor in terms of global warming, and in the process we are forcing them to collude with us in feeding our excesses. The responsibility to provide farmers in the South with an alternative, sustainable, source of income and food for themselves, is inescapably ours.

Localised food production, not just in relation to meat, is a global imperative. It is no use our protesting that food costs more at farmers' markets, or complaining when strawberries are not available in the middle of winter. If we are ever to take global warming seriously, the emissions involved in producing and transporting our food just have to be cut.

Food offered to idols?

Michael Northcott, in his book *A Moral Climate*, has a trenchant view of modern food production and our consumption of it:

> The contemporary form of idolatry is the devotion of the culture of food to money, from crop to table. This produces a new kind of profanity in which industrial food is debased while the soil is eroded, the land poisoned and the climate changed. By participating without critique in the fruits of modern agronomy, do Christians analogously 'eat meat offered to idols' and imbibe a worldview which is contrary to the Gospel?[12]

Northcott goes on to claim that food is politics and that the Eucharist is therefore political food. He argues that this food involves sacrifices – of the soil, healthy rural communities and the climate. Just as Martelet sees in the eucharistic elements symbols of the world's distress, so Northcott brings a sharp political dimension to the Lord's Table.

Maybe sacred Christian symbolism is a good place to start. Most Christian congregations would find it something of a challenge to bring to the Eucharist elements that are entirely locally sourced. Some will complain that 'it isn't the same'. But in our efforts to do that we would be breaking the link of consumerism and essential human nourishment. How can people of faith then not take that principle forward in their own lives and out into the wider world?

Indigenous peoples' right to life

It has become increasingly apparent in recent years that indigenous peoples in regions from the South Pacific to the Americas and the Arctic regions are particularly vulnerable to climate change. Their traditional ways of living have long been under threat, and the additional impact of global warming on their land, forest and marine resources brings with it the loss of homes and livelihoods. So, for example, deforestation in South America has destroyed forest-dwelling communities, while rising temperatures in the Arctic have led to the loss of access to traditional hunting and fishing grounds thanks to unsafe and melting ice, and lethal mud-slides have wiped out homes. If this was happening to citizens in virtually any other part of the world, the outcry would be deafening.

Declaration on the Rights of Indigenous Peoples (Resolution adopted by the UN General Assembly, October 2007)
This declaration establishes a universal framework of minimum standards for the survival, dignity, well-being and rights of the world's indigenous peoples. (Four states voted against the adoption of the Resolution: Australia, New Zealand, the United States and Canada.) Articles relevant to their current vulnerability include:

- *Article 10:* Indigenous peoples shall not be forcibly removed from their lands or territories. No relocation shall take place without the free, prior and informed consent of the indigenous peoples concerned and after agreement on just and fair compensation and, where possible, with the option of return.
- *Article 18:* Indigenous peoples have the right to participate in decision-making in matters which would affect their own rights ...
- *Article 23:* Indigenous peoples have the right to determine and develop priorities and strategies for exercising their right to development.
- *Article 24:* Indigenous peoples have the right to their traditional medicines and to maintain their health practices, including the conservation of their vital medicinal plants, animals and minerals.
- *Article 32:* Indigenous peoples have the right to determine and develop priorities and strategies for the

> development or use of their lands or territories and
> other resources.

For indigenous peoples, the threat to their right to life and to
a home is more than a matter of physical survival. Their
social life and culture – things that people in most countries
take for granted – is in jeopardy and, in the case of traditional
knowledge and medicinal plants, has already been shame-
lessly plundered by large drug companies for their own
financial ends.

The situation of indigenous peoples is a clear example of
initiatives designed to halt climate change creating new
injustices. For example, there is no reference to their rights in
the new international programme on Reducing Emissions
from Deforestation and Forest Degradation (REDD), carbon
trading is contributing to the degradation of their environment, and some Clean Development Mechanism projects
have led to the deaths of people refusing to hand over their
territories.[13]

A full discussion of the situation of indigenous peoples is
beyond the scope of this book, but I have included reference
to it here for two reasons: first, because such people seem to
me to encapsulate both the injustice of climate change (they
have done next to nothing to cause it) and the potential
injustice of many of the ways forward that are being proposed; and second, perhaps because of their very invisibility
to so many of us, their predicament is a searing indictment of

our failure to love our neighbour. As Christians we have much to learn from them not only in terms of lifestyle but also in terms of their spirituality.[14] Yet their hope for the future seems to reside in the effectiveness (or otherwise) of international human rights conventions. Christians who are unhappy with that, need urgently to consider what they are going to do instead.

No easy way out

The letter to the church at Pergamum reminds us that there is no avoiding the hard issues and no easy way out. The church is told that unless it changes its ways pretty quickly, there will be trouble: 'I will come to you soon and make war against them with the sword of my mouth' (Rev. 2:16). Today's Church must open its eyes to the full consequences of our actions, as they affect people remote from us, and understand that those people's lives and our spiritual integrity are both at risk.

Questions for discussion

1. Human rights: profoundly Christian principles or a secular blueprint to do what you want?
2. Climate change involves all of us in hard choices. Which

are the ones confronting you now and how are you dealing with them?

Chapter 5

Trade, Development and Conservation

> *Q:* If the UK begins the calendar year with the same amount of
> energy that Tanzania will use in the whole of that year, when
> will it run out?
> *A:* At 20.00 hours on January 3rd.[1]

Thyatira: tolerating Jezebel (Rev. 2:18–29)

'Love, faith, service and patient endurance' (Rev. 2:19) – the
qualities of the church at Thyatira would seem to put it
almost above reproach. There was just one problem: like so
many others, this church was guilty of excessive compromise
with its non-Christian context. We should not be distracted
by John's evocative imagery with its references to fornication.
The church had not become a haven for sexual immorality.
Rather, it was allowing in its midst an advocate of pagan
worship and practice; so for all its virtues, the church was
indulging in nothing less than religious infidelity, allowing its
faith to be contaminated by non-Christian activities. And this
was down to one thing: economics, and in particular international trade.

Thyatira lay at a strategic point in the communications

system of the Roman Empire, on the road between Perga-mum and Laodicea. It was an important centre of manu-facturing, including the metal-working that John alludes to in his reference to the feet of the Son of God being like 'burn-ished bronze' (v. 18). And as a result it was also home to a large number of trade guilds. And while these, like their medieval counterparts, served an important commercial and social purpose, membership of them entailed the acceptance of pagan practices of one form or another. (There is an example of this in Acts 19, where silversmiths are engaged in the highly profitable activity of making shrines of Artemis. Here the guild exerts its considerable collective power in responding violently to Paul's challenge of their trade.)

The historical figure of Jezebel was a symbol of religious compromise. Her marriage to Ahab (1 Kings 16:31) cemen-ted the trading alliance between Israel and Phoenicia (with its great trading port of Tyre), and Jezebel brought with her the full panoply of Baal worship. This led eventually to God's punishment on Ahab's descendants. So the force of John's accusation that the church at Thyatira is tolerating Jezebel should not be underestimated: it is nothing short of shocking.

The letter to Thyatira is also not untypical of the suspicion with which the Bible, the Old Testament in particular, regards trade. Much of that, of course, has to do with Israel's history and its uncomfortable transition from an agricultural to a manufacturing economy. The consequences of this for Israel's relationship with God, as people start to embrace the values and practices of their trading partners, are reflected in such passages as Ezekiel's elaborate and detailed proclamations against Tyre (Ezek. 27). And while it is important to remember that honest trade *per se* is perfectly acceptable, the necessarily close working relationships that it entails are not always compatible with religious observance.

Trade, economics and climate change

In late 2006 a bulky report for the UK Government by Sir Nicholas Stern, former Chief Economist of the World Bank, hit the headlines with its claim that it would cost less to tackle climate change than it would to ignore it:

> The world does not need to choose between averting climate change and promoting growth and development. Changes in energy technologies and in the structure of economies have created opportunities to decouple growth from greenhouse gas emissions. Indeed, ignoring climate change will eventually damage economic growth. Tackling climate change is the pro-growth strategy for the longer term, and it can be done in a way that does not cap the aspirations for growth of rich or poor countries.[2]

How climate change may be tackled is key here. Not surprisingly, there has been enthusiastic acceptance of the idea that climate change is simply another problem that technology will be able to solve, with all that this implies for investment and profit. And it is tempting to think that this lets us all off the hook. Sadly, the reality is rather different. Research and development of new technologies takes many years, and we cannot be certain that the right solution will emerge at the end of it. Equally, the effects of some of the technological fixes that have been proposed are largely unknown. One example is carbon capture and storage (CCS) whereby carbon is stored beneath the sea. No one knows what the long-term effects of this may be, always assuming it proves to be possible in the first place.

A simple, not to say simplistic, response would be to argue that instead of pandering to our instincts to preserve our comfortable status quo, and trusting industry to save the planet for us, we need to wake up fast to our responsibilities as individuals and as communities. After all, the selfishness that impels us to hang on to what we've got (and in the process to deny it to other people) is neither moral nor Christian. But that said, the urgency of the issue means that we need all the help we can get, and it would be foolish to reject technological possibilities out of hand. But maybe there are other ways forward as well.

Trading carbon

Besides proposed technological solutions to climate change, there are also the economic incentives devised to encourage a reduction in carbon emissions, the best known and also the most complicated of them being carbon trading. This concept was a key feature of the Kyoto Protocol and, put very simply, this works a bit like carbon offsetting: countries are allocated a specific number of carbon credits, and once they have used them they purchase more from countries that have some to spare. Like offsetting, it is the rich who benefit, this time from the notional emissions of poor countries which their lack of development prevents them from using themselves. For developed nations and their deep-rooted adherence to illiberal trading practices, carbon trading is an attractive option, and institutions such as international carbon exchanges are already in place.

Carbon trading in the EU
The EU emissions trading scheme (known as EU ETS) works like a traditional stock market, with the price of carbon fluctuating according to supply and demand. For example, a cold and dry winter in Scandinavia would result in little hydro-power being available, and more coal being used, which would push up the price of carbon. A mild wet winter, on the other hand, would bring down the price accordingly.

Each country is given a legally binding emissions target and meeting that target may depend on buying credits from another. Unsurprisingly, the emissions allowances for each country are hotly debated, and four of the 25 EU States have so far not signed up to the scheme at all.

Economic alternatives

A Green New Deal

The Green New Deal Group that first met in 2007 is made up of experts in the fields of finance, energy and environmental issues. It is working on policies to solve what it calls the 'triple crunch' of the credit crisis, climate change and high oil prices.[3] The group's aim is to promote joined-up thinking about the four systems that dominate our world – the market, the state, civil society and the ecosystems, and their hope is that it will lay the foundations for a radical transformation and renewal of our financial, political and ecosystems.

A Green New Deal: regulation and market enablement

The first report of the Green New Deal Group revisits the three major planks of Roosevelt's 1930s New Deal in the aftermath of the Great Depression:

- Regulation of the financial sector.
- Providing funding for infrastructure (especially through increased taxation of big businesses and the rich).

- Investment in a wide range of infrastructural projects, including training, in order to get people back to work and generate business opportunities (and in the 1930s this included environmental programmes).

The Green New Deal proposes a bigger role for investments from private savings, banks and insurance. The climate change-related proposals are twofold:

- Decarbonisation, beginning with the electricity supply industry, with investment matched by increased efficiency and conservation by users and suppliers.
- Serious investment in building new energy-supply systems (including energy efficiency and renewables).

This will be achieved by:

- A new legislative framework backed up by rising carbon taxes, higher prices for traded carbon and a big increase in investment in energy infrastructure.

This is what life in a time of global warming will soon be looking like: higher taxes, a transformed renewable energy sector and serious energy-saving requirements made of all of us; but also new commercial opportunities that should benefit communities both in the developed and in the developing worlds. And there is the opportunity too for faith communities to take a hard look at the ethics that will be driving these new initiatives and to make their voices heard sooner rather than later, to advocate ways of working together without compromise.

Greenhouse Development Rights (GDRs)

Another way forward is proposed in a new approach to the global climate regime by EcoEquity and Christian Aid. This calls on rich countries to provide the resources that would allow society to move to clean, efficient, low-carbon economies. It allocates obligations to nations according to their responsibility (their historic contribution to the climate problem) and capacity (their ability to dedicate resources to the problem). Importantly, it imposes parallel obligations on developing countries. Recognising that there are considerable disparities in wealth within some developing countries (India and South Africa, for example), it calculates national obligations in a way that is sensitive to this income structure.

This approach, which is attracting increasing international interest, is intended as a frame of reference: a standard of comparison between what is happening and what is urgently needed. It demands commitments from nations above and beyond what they currently seem inclined to accept, and illustrates just how costly this change is going to be.[4]

Overseas development: doing things differently

The imbalance in energy resources in developed and developing countries is starkly conveyed in the contrast between Tanzania and the UK at the start of this chapter. Yet, as I have already stressed, we cannot allow global warming to stand in the way of enabling countries like Tanzania to continue on their development path. Development must not be halted but it will need to be done differently if there is to be a significant reduction in global carbon emissions. Already, NGOs have been active in getting renewable energy supplies into areas that have hitherto had no power supply. We have already seen how some countries (including Tanzania) skipped a stage in telecommunications technology by largely bypassing telephone landlines and moving straight into mobile telephony, with the result that in some developing countries mobiles seem to be as common as they are in the UK. We shall hopefully see the same pattern being followed in other technologies, which should enable development to move forward at a significant pace.

There has been a lot of talk in the past few years about adaptation funds for developing countries. Adaptation has to do with reducing the harm, or risk of harm, associated with climate change (as opposed to 'mitigation', which is about addressing the causes of climate change – for example, by reducing carbon emissions). In addition, there is the whole question of carbon offsetting, a process by which companies and individuals make a contribution to a suitable environmental project in order to 'offset' or 'compensate for' the carbon that they are generating themselves, typically through flights.

It is already a cliché in church circles to compare offsetting to the medieval practice of the sale of indulgences: you can continue with your harmful activities if you're prepared to pay for them. Many people will say that they distrust offsetting projects, not accepting that any scheme that involves transferring cash to projects (whether at home or, more likely, overseas) also involves administrative costs. And it is undoubtedly the case that some offsetting projects that have sprung up are decidedly dodgy. But there is good offsetting and bad offsetting, and good offsetting is, in my view, very much better than no offsetting at all, although it has the moral downside that it is an option limited to people who can afford it.

There is potentially a great deal of money available worldwide for adaptation projects and, not surprisingly, there are a number of challenges that arise from this. One principle that has been repeatedly stressed within the UNFCCC conferences is that funding must be genuinely new money: it is not acceptable that, say, government development aid is simply relabelled 'climate change adaptation'. Then there are the vexed questions of distribution of funding (with virtually every country considering itself hard done by), which projects should qualify for funding, and who should benefit. That last question is particularly relevant in the context of international development, as it is imperative that poor people should benefit from adaptation processes.

Much climate change work in the developing world will build on so-called 'disaster risk reduction' processes of mitigation – for example, strengthening homes and public buildings to reduce the impact of cyclones. However, researchers at the International Development Institute of the University of Sussex have argued that climate change adaptation may also present developmental opportunities, by providing ways out of chronic poverty that go beyond tackling the additional impacts of climate change. Examples include changes to ecosystems to make them more productive and transitions to labour-intensive biofuel crops.[5]

Civil war, deforestation and land erosion: the case of Bujumbura

The environmental crisis in Burundi is due to a combination of factors, which have been aggravated by climate change. The ten-year civil war, which ended in 2003, was responsible for extensive deforestation, as rebel and government troops cut down forests in order to flush out the enemy. This resulted in bare hillsides, as well as the loss of much agricultural land.

Climate change has led to a disruption in weather patterns, particularly rainfall. There is now very heavy rainfall at unseasonal times, resulting in floods. This flooding is causing severe slides of mud and rocks down the bare hills, with the result that smallholdings and homes are ruined, rivers polluted and bridges destroyed. Water pollution means that women have to walk miles to buy water at the nearest market, although most poor people will simply take the polluted water from the river.

The loss of agricultural land and produce has severe consequences for the capital Bujumbura, since Burundi is already suffering from food shortages. Remedies being actively pursued are re-forestation, help for farmers to protect their land from mudslides and the rebuilding of roads and bridges.

Developing cities

In a stimulating question and answer session following a lecture I'd given to an Oxford University student audience on climate change in Africa, I was slightly taken aback to be asked whether overseas development discriminated against the urban poor. It was a good question, because so much development work is focused on the very poorest communities, who do indeed tend to be in rural areas. There is, of course, a great deal of work also going on in the cities of some of the poorest countries. But if there is an imbalance, global warming demands that it is redressed and even tilted in the other direction.

In a report on climate change and cities, the International Institute for Environment and Development (IIED) argues that the future development of cities in Africa, Asia and Latin America will be one of the main influences on future greenhouse gas emissions.[6] This is not to say that all that needs to be done is to encourage low-carbon lifestyles in the cities of poor countries as well as the rich ones. The situation is more complicated than that for several reasons.

First, there is the vulnerability of many cities in developing countries. Coastal cities are at risk from sea-level rises and also from the lethal combination of storm surges and high tides. The fast-growing cities of South-East Asia are particularly vulnerable, with rising water levels undermining the foundations of buildings and putting at risk tourism infrastructure that is vital to the economy of the region. Inland cities, located beside rivers or in the foothills of mountains, are at risk of flooding and subsequent water pollution, and water shortages resulting from glacier melt. And their economies are also at risk from the effects of extreme weather on agricultural production in the surrounding countryside.

Then secondly, the poorest cities lack the capacity to adapt to global warming. It is estimated that there are up to one billion slum-dwellers worldwide, and in many places, much of the city's labour force, maybe up to half the population, lives in informal settlements that are at greatest risk from storms and floods. The IIED authors argue that without fundamental changes in the way in which city governments work with low-income populations, effective adaptation to climate change is impossible. They conclude:

> Investments in adaptation must work with low-income groups. This means fully involving them in plans to reduce flooding and other risks. Relocating those living in informal settlements should be avoided wherever possible. Instead, upgrading programmes should be favoured, in which governments work with the inhabitants to combine improved infrastructure – for instance, for water, sanitation and drainage – with risk reduction.

These are all considerations for development specialists to take into account, in addition to their traditional role of enabling poor people to have sustainable livelihoods. Poverty reduction now means more than providing a source of income: it means reducing the environmental risk to which the urban poor are vulnerable, through improved infrastructure and a greater awareness on the part of city councils of effective local adaptation. And cities themselves must also take responsibility, by putting in place mechanisms for good governance, including, for example, procedures for holding government officials to account after disasters.

People with holes in their feet[7]

Kenya has become increasingly vulnerable to drought and water scarcity. In summer, the Nairobi river, that runs through the centre of the capital and out through one of the densely populated slum areas, is now little more than a muddy stream. It's ironic that 'Nairobi' means 'clean, fresh water' because this river is anything but clean. As it passes through the Korogocho slum, it scoops up waste from the city's dump site, in addition to the chemical effluent discharged by local industry.

The dump site, situated within the boundaries of the city, is where the worst waste material is deposited – anything obviously recyclable has already been removed. Yet the slum dwellers, the poorest people in the city, work ceaselessly to recover what they can from this stinking mass of waste, in a desperate attempt to rework it into something they can sell. Because the river separates their shacks from the dump, people are forced to wade through its polluted water. The effect is devastating for human health. As an Italian Catholic priest, who has chosen to make his own home in Korogocho, commented: 'When we wash people's feet at the Maundy Thursday service, we see that those feet have holes in them'.

Restoring the forests

The natural capacity of trees and vegetation to absorb carbon dioxide has resulted in tree planting becoming a remedy of choice for local communities in the UK and in many other places. But planting trees virtually indiscriminately is only a short-term fix. As we have already seen, a tree once cut down releases carbon that becomes CO_2, and this basically is why deforestation accounts for as much as 22 per cent of carbon dioxide emissions worldwide. It is also a strategy that has provoked hostility in some parts of the world, with some African nations angrily claiming that offset schemes that plant trees in their regions are simply using them as 'carbon sinks' – a means of absorbing the ongoing emissions of the North. In addition, scientists are telling us that whereas vegetation has up to now absorbed around 50 per cent of industrial emissions, there are signs that this is breaking down and plants no longer seem able to absorb so much. So planting trees is, it seems, no substitute for reducing emissions.

Nonetheless it remains important to restore forests that have been cut down, not only because of the carbon dioxide they absorb but because less forest means less rain in drought-prone areas and because, as in the case of Burundi featured above, having fewer trees leads to disastrous land erosion and exposure to other climate hazards. In some countries as well, legislation has resulted in a clamp-down on illegal tree-cutting. But it is important to ensure that these worthy processes do not add to the burden of poor people. I have heard an emotional plea from an Indonesian lady protesting that illegal loggers were not bad people – they simply had no other way of surviving. And what about poor people around the world who depend on the nearest forests for firewood and a source of cooking fuel? If the natural balance of things is to be restored, or begin to be restored, that has to involve relationships between people as well as their relationship with the natural world.

Bamtaare

In northern Senegal around two-thirds of the population live on less than $2 a day. It's a flat dry and sandy region and the Sahara is only 50km to the north of the northern border. Since 1972, when there was a severe drought, there has been a general lack of rain and that has caused a steady loss of trees which in turn makes the region drier still. People can measure this very precisely: in one village the wood used to be a few metres' walk away, but now the villagers have to take a cart 15km to find some. Climatic factors and a lack of government support for agriculture have combined to keep the poorest people poor. But some things can be remedied. To help overcome this lack of wood, in some villages a local NGO has provided energy efficient stoves and also taught people how to make them. The change is dramatic. With a traditional stove it used to

---

take three to four hours to cook 5kg of rice, using 14 pieces of wood. With an energy efficient stove it takes only an hour and a half and just three pieces of wood, and of course there's less smoke as well, while people spend much less time looking for wood and can economise on their use of it. These stoves are very basic, constructed out of clay, straw, cow dung and old tins. In the local language they are called 'Bamtaare' meaning 'a harmonious development which considers the lives of all people and the environment for a collective, sustainable and lasting development'!

Christian Aid internal report 2006

Carbon and conservation

The Rio Earth Summit of 1992 adopted the Convention on Biological Diversity, providing a legal framework for biodiversity conservation. In its broadest sense, biodiversity is about life on earth, and although it is popularly supposed to relate to the plant and animal world, it is also about people and our need for food security, shelter and a clean and healthy environment in which to live.

Restoring the forests is a crucial element both in reducing carbon dioxide emissions and in preserving biodiversity (including the environment of forest-dwelling peoples). It is also cheap and becomes effective relatively quickly. Since Bali it has been widely argued that the next international climate change agreement must include measures to reduce deforestation in tropical countries. This naturally gives rise not only to reforestation, but also to afforestation (new plantations) and the prevention of further deforestation through sustainable forest management and establishing protected areas.

Conservation funds are a long-standing alternative to carbon trading, and money for them is likely to increase considerably if REDD ('reduced emissions from deforestation and degradation') projects are included in the post-2012 international agreement. However, like adaptation funding, it must be ensured that this represents new money and not cash recycled from other sources. Among significant projects already in place is a fund to help conserve the Congo Basin rainforest.

'Weeping and mourning for Babylon the Great'

The imagery used in the letter to Thyatira crops up again in Revelation 18, with the graphic description of the fall of Babylon. Here, though, the metaphor of fornication is much more clearly identified with people's seduction into the false religion associated with trade and economic prosperity. So while Revelation 16 portrays the full horror of progressive environmental destruction, the fate of Babylon is accomplished in a stroke: 'her plagues will come in a single day – pestilence and mourning and famine – and she will be burned with fire' (18:8). The city is mourned by the merchants and seafarers whose economic interests depended on her (vv. 11–19) and no one can escape destruction, whether or not they have any responsibility for it: 'the light of a lamp will shine in you no more; and the voice of bridegroom and bride will be heard in you no more' (v. 23). The city has seduced merchants and nations, with the consequent martyrdom of 'prophets and saints' (v. 24) – that is, the faithful who have opposed compromise with pagan values.

We have now to hope that our love affair with economic prosperity is not beyond redemption. It should be possible to engage with political processes such as those outlined in *A Green New Deal* while at the same time reining in our excessive consumerism. Our hope has to be that we will find a more clearly defined Christian way of living 'in the world' without becoming 'of the world'.

Questions for discussion

1. Think of the city that is nearest to where you live or work. What might it look like in 20, 30 or 50 years' time, at different stages in its 'decarbonisation'?
2. How will your family's lifestyle change over a similar period?

Chapter 6

An Open Door

Philadelphia and its patient endurance
(Rev. 3:7–13)

Philadelphia was a city in an earthquake zone. It was destroyed in AD 17 (as indeed was Sardis) and although it was rebuilt, many of its citizens were too frightened to return. So John's vision of permanence and stability (v. 12) would have been particularly attractive to them.

Although small, Philadelphia was a faithful church, despite the false accusations from 'the synagogue of Satan' to which it was subject. It may be that the 'open door' set before the faithful ('Look, I have set before you an open door, which no one is able to shut', v. 8) represents opportunities for conversion, despite the hostility that surrounded them, and the same metaphor is used several times in the Pauline epistles. I would, though, prefer to see it as Jesus himself, echoing the 'I am' sayings of John's Gospel: 'I am the gate of the sheep ... Whoever enters by me will be saved, and will come in and go out and find pasture' (John 10:7, 9). In other words, Jesus himself is ever present to offer refuge to his beleaguered people.

The letter to Philadelphia will have a particular resonance for today's communities that are vulnerable to natural disasters, whether or not these are climate-related. The Philadelphian church had experienced at first hand not only the physical devastation caused by an earthquake, but also its effects on the lives of local people, most notably their displacement to surrounding areas. They knew too that this was not an isolated event. In that area there would be more earthquakes and more human suffering. Patient endurance was an attitude of mind in the face of the hostility of nature as much as in confronting the hostility of the local Jewish population.

So perhaps the open door has here a multiple significance: a safe refuge from the danger of the elements and from human persecution, as well as a spiritual sanctuary for the Christian faithful and for those in search of truth.

This short chapter looks at two particularly difficult issues. The first is one of the most distressing consequences of climate change, the plight of environmental refugees. The other is the challenge of population growth, which I shall consider briefly afterwards.

Already we can see patient endurance exemplified in people of regions that are vulnerable to rising sea levels, as they are forced to move further and further inland, draining their resources when they had little enough to start with. And already the challenge to be an open door is confronting not only cities such as Dhaka, whose sizeable slum population is being swollen by poor people fleeing the coastal regions of Bangladesh, but also other countries and other continents. The pressure on southern Europe to receive people from sub-Saharan Africa is considerable. It will only increase as many more Africans are forced out of their countries by drought as well as by economic hardship. Yet parts of southern Europe too are drying up. It is not impossible that before long we shall see great migrations of people northwards through Europe, with similar movements of populations in South-East Asia, the South Pacific and across central America. Whose doors will remain open then?

Climate change and migration

In 2005 the United Nations warned that environmental factors, in particular rising sea levels, desertification and shrinking fresh-water supplies, were displacing up to 10 million people a year. Their concern was echoed by the Red Cross, claiming that environmental disasters were already displacing more people than war. One particular issue is the fact that these migrants are not recognised under international agreements as refugees, so they cannot be treated in the same way as people seeking asylum for other reasons such as political persecution.

Furthermore, it may not be easy to distinguish between economic and environmental refugees, not least because poor people are also those most adversely affected by global warming. They may not distinguish between the two themselves, seeing environmental change as just one more thing making their lives difficult, or perhaps as simply the last straw. Nonetheless, many people do know all too well that they would not be leaving their homes if it were not for the changing climate.

Climate change in Mali

Oumou Karembe, aged 76, has four sons and four daughters. More than enough to look after her in her old age, she thought. But that was in the days when enough rain fell to sustain the farmers living in Africa's Sahel region. After the massive droughts of the early 1980s, Oumou's village never fully recovered. Indeed, since then, the rain has become less and less predictable. Two years ago, the last of Oumou's sons was forced to leave the remote village in northern Mali because he could no longer feed his family with what he was able to grow ...

'One by one my children asked permission to leave', said Oumou's husband, Ibrahim. 'Every time they didn't come

---

back, it was a shock. But with the changing climate it would be difficult for them all to stay here.'

During the past five years, farmers have reported rain disappearing in the middle of the growing season, which drastically reduces, if not totally destroys, their crops. This change in rainfall patterns is creating a new wave of migrants who are being driven from their homes in search of water, leaving the very old and the very young in the villages to cope as best they can. Already the third poorest country in the world, the fragile Malian economy is facing yet another shock.

Christian Aid[1]

In Mali, 70 per cent of the population live in rural areas. Since people generally don't want to leave their homes, the first and best solution is to find a way to enable them to stay while at the same time helping them not just to maintain but to improve their standard of living. So the Mali government is encouraging farmers to use drought-resistant strains of crops. They are also training villagers to gather their own rainfall data so that they can make the best use of the rain that does fall.

A further possibility is to grow alternative crops such as jatropha, which can be used as a biofuel. It also helps to prevent soil erosion when it is growing. This does not present the same ethical problem as the production of biofuels described in Chapter 3, since no food crops have been cleared to make way for it. It is seen as a potential source of local employment and income, and since Mali depends on imported fossil fuel, its importance in the development of clean energy is considerable.

Migration of people from rural Mali has helped to raise the population in the capital Bamako to more than double what it was 20 years ago. This has led to security problems and an increase of HIV, and is forcing people to contemplate the dangerous route of migration to Europe. The most common route is overland through Mauritania and a boat crossing to Spain, where the virtual impossibility of getting a visa means that people are sent back the same way. Clearly the preferred way forward is radical change in Mali itself. If that policy fails, Europe will need not only to provide an open door but to offer a safe passage to it as well.

It does not take much to reverse the trend to migration in at least some small communities. Since a dam was installed in Zoungou in Burkina Faso to counteract the increasingly irregular rainfall, there has been a significant increase in agricultural productivity and a return to two harvests a year. This has had the effect of halting migration. Where previously people were leaving for Ghana or the neighbouring Ivory Coast, now at least some young people are remaining in the area and a few have even returned from the Ivory Coast.

Rising sea levels

Probably the area currently most at risk from rising sea levels, and also the best known, is Tuvalu, with its nine small islands in the South Pacific. Ironically, Tuvalu is on the brink of a small economic explosion, thanks to the opening up of website domain names (Tuvalu has the rights to its country suffix, .tv). But this will count for nothing if sea levels continue to rise. This has resulted in the erosion of coastal soil and the saline contamination of agricultural land and drinking water. Without the water and crops that they need to sustain their very basic lifestyle, it is likely that the 10,000 or so Tuvaluans will become the first entire nation of environmental refugees. Yet despite the very strong probability that Tuvalu and other island states will suffer irreversible damage in the next two decades, and despite a call to governments from the Pacific Council of Churches to focus on resettlement, there seem as yet to be no plans in place for the future, beyond a promise from New Zealand to accept the Tuvaluans.

The IPCC has highlighted the vast numbers of people around the world who are at risk from flooding by the sea: 'In the absence of an improvement to protection, coastal flooding could grow tenfold or more by the 2080s to [affect] more than 100 million people a year, just due to sea-level rise alone.'[2] And while this may seem to be quite a remote problem, we should not forget our vulnerability in the UK as islands, nor that even here the sea has risen by 10 cm in the last century.

Security

In a speech to the Thirteenth Economic Forum in Prague back in May 2005, Professor Norman Myers of Oxford University drew attention to the link between environmental refugees and national security. He saw much of this as centred on the limits to the capacity and willingness to take in outsiders, and the tensions and civil disorder that are likely to result. A couple of years later Professor Robert McLeman of the University of Ottawa focused his concerns on the regions most vulnerable to climate change: 'Regions where climate change holds the greatest risk of creating population displacement include countries that are already wracked by conflict and are hosts to groups that pose security concerns internally and internationally.'[3] Given that the conflict in areas such as Darfur has been intensified (and some would say even caused) by food and water shortages resulting from climate change, the consequences of the additional pressure of populations on the move in these regions are almost unthinkable.

Population: the elephant in the room?

It is not unknown for Christian pastors to advise couples that it is their duty to have children in order to produce more Christians in an unbelieving world. In a free society it will, of course, never follow that children wholeheartedly espouse their parents' belief. God's command to 'be fruitful and multiply' (Gen. 9.7) underlies the subsequent development of the nation of Israel at a time when population growth was necessary for survival and is not necessarily appropriate in a modern context. And the prayer in the Christian marriage service for the couple to be blessed with children is optional (although generally only so when the woman is 'past child-bearing age'). With previously undreamt-of medical advances both in birth control and human fertility, the human race should have little difficulty in determining its own number. But the seemingly intractable moral problem is whether it should, how it should, and who decides.

Until very recently, the subject of population control has been largely taboo. Like all taboos, this has to do with fear: a fear of appearing to approve of totalitarian regimes that have oppressively enforced one-child-per-family policies; a fear of being accused of contemplating Nazi-style atrocities; a fear of unacceptable interference in other people's lives. Yet in most debates, whether secular or church-based, the question of population control is almost always raised, and the answers given are never satisfactory, not mine or anyone else's.

It is important to bear in mind that family size is regarded very differently from one culture to another. Where hard-up parents in the UK may see another child as another mouth to feed, parents in India (for example) will welcome another pair of hands to enable the family to earn a living. When two such cultures collide, racist overtones start to creep in. Increasing immigration has, in the case of the UK, contributed to racist attitudes, as immigrants are perceived as bringing large numbers of children into the country or continuing their large-family traditions in a host country that is already overcrowded. This fear of racism has surely added to the reluctance of government and religious institutions alike to confront the issue, and with the prospect of increasing migration due to environmental changes, the elephant in the room is growing larger almost by the day.

The fear that our planet cannot sustain uncontrolled human population growth has been made more acute by global warming. More human beings will simply add to the impact of climate change, at least in the developed North. And maybe this is the heart of the issue. More children in a UK family will lead eventually, in the majority of cases, to more cars on the road. The same cannot be said for a family in Africa or Asia, where the change to a family's, or even a community's, carbon footprint is at present likely to be negligible.

But maybe population figures will in the long run prove to be a distraction from the very much more urgent need to reduce greenhouse gas emissions. Just as we are beginning to hear more voices calling for at least some debate on the subject of population, others are more cautiously optimistic, because as the world's population grows (at the time of writing it stood at around 6.7 billion),[4] birth rates are falling. According to the Oxford demographer Professor David Coleman, the global population is likely to peak at 9.5 billion by 2050, and will begin to decline around 2070.[5] The social reasons for this projection are fascinating but not directly relevant to the climate change debate. What we must not lose sight of is that people (and their carbon footprints) are living longer, that more people in the developing world are likely to have significantly larger carbon footprints in the future, and that the need for affordable food will become greater in the immediate future.

If there is anything approaching a population crisis, global warming inevitably will make matters worse. With increasing population numbers, even if only temporarily, will come greater food and housing needs – a situation which is further complicated by the loss of homes and agricultural land due to climate-related factors. In the developing world, greater demands for technology will need to be met by much improved and much cheaper green technologies, and there will be countless challenges in terms of the provision of medical services, education and so on.

For parents or would-be parents who have a genuine choice about the size of their families, the well-being of the planet would seem to be a more worthy consideration than the desire to populate the world with right-minded Christians. If religion has any part at all to play in what must, in the interests of human rights and freedoms, surely remain the choice of the individual, it might be to downplay the traditional view that large families are a blessing – a view that is shared by Christians, Muslims, Hindus and others. It would be another small step in repairing our fractured relationship with the natural world.

Apocalypse soon?

It may be significant that Philadelphia is the only church of the seven to be warned of what lies ahead: 'the hour of trial that is coming on the whole world' (Rev. 3:10). It may also be worth remembering that this is letter number six, given the symbolic significance of that number in apocalyptic writing – 666 and all that. If this makes the letter to the Philadelphians particularly portentous, the whole subject of environmental refugees is surely no less so. How we treat one another in the face of extreme weather events worldwide will be a test of our humanity. If we fail that test, we may as well abandon all our efforts to reduce greenhouse gasses. Because, to put it very starkly, we won't be worth saving.

Questions for discussion

1. Imagine that environmental refugees have increased the size of your local community by at least 50 per cent. What will be the problems and the benefits? How will this affect the work of the local church?
2. Population growth: should it be controlled? If so, how and by whom? And if not, why not?

Chapter 7

Living with Global Warming

If you have blue suede shoes with a large carbon footprint like
a rock band, then it's difficult.
              Rock star and anti-poverty campaigner Bono[1]

At last, you may think, the practical action chapter that will
help people like Bono reduce their carbon footprint. Sorry,
it's not. There are more than enough publications around
offering advice on a greener lifestyle, along with more specialist topics such as lobbying MPs or environmental Bible
studies, without my adding to them. What this chapter aims
to do is to change the emphasis. I want to move on from all
the ideas about how we can combat climate change, which
can so easily suggest that the crisis is not yet with us and can
be delayed. Instead I would like to look at what it means to be
living through that crisis: how do we live in a way that is
appropriate to what is going on around us, and in particular,
how does global warming affect different aspects of our life as
a Church? What is now different about the life of the people
of God?[2]

Sardis: the inoffensive church

Like the church at Laodicea, the Christian community in Sardis, once the capital city of Croesus, enjoyed considerable prosperity, although John does not treat it with quite the same negativity. Unlike Laodicea, the church at Sardis had a good reputation; there is no hint that it blows neither hot nor cold. But John's accusation is that it is living off its good name. Sardis was not troubled by heretics, false prophets or hostile Jewish groups. And in that comfortable environment the church was a pretty inoffensive institution. It appeared to be alive and thriving, but spiritually it was dead. The vital impulse to challenge the surrounding culture just wasn't there.

Out of the seven churches Sardis is perhaps the one with which it is easiest to draw contemporary parallels. It is a church that is there if it's needed, but it looks after itself sufficiently well not to bother outsiders with fund-raising appeals or other troublesome initiatives. Peaceful co-existence is its motto, which means that any mission activity or any challenges to the social status quo are at best muted. Hence the criticism in verse 2, 'I have not found your works perfect in the sight of my God', an accusation that Caird translates as 'Nothing you do is ever completed in the eyes of God'.[3] There are a lot of good ideas but they don't quite get put into practice; there is little about the inoffensive church to trouble its peace-loving and affluent neighbours.

This lack of spiritual vitality has serious consequences. While the church at Sardis is not called to martyrdom, it is reminded of its call to 'walk with' Christ, to share in the suffering of Jesus in order to share in his glory. 'Everyone who acknowledges me before others, the Son of Man will also acknowledge before the angels of God', says Jesus (Luke 12:8), but being inoffensive is not a good starting point.

How, then, is today's Church, which in very many places has made inoffensiveness into an art form, to put that comfortable philosophy aside and to set about living effectively through the crisis of climate change?

'A shared community'

We have put aside our religious differences to focus on what we share in common: an understanding that global climate change is threatening our world and a commitment to do something about it.

This statement comes from a 2008 initiative in the United States called the Genesis Covenant. Its mission is to ask every religious group to sign a public agreement, that every facility they own will reduce their greenhouse gas emissions by a minimum of 50 per cent in ten years. Under the headings of 'a shared vision', 'a shared response', 'a shared action', and 'a shared community', the Genesis Covenant declares that the time for discussing climate change is over and that it is time for action. And one significant element is that it can only be signed by *national* religious bodies, such as the American Episcopal Church, which plans to take this step in 2009. In other words, not only is the time for climate change denial well past. So too is individual action which is by implication ineffective unless it is contributing to a much bigger movement. The Genesis Covenant calls for commitment by people of faith *in community*.

The emphasis on community is crucial. Individuals on their own won't make much difference to climate change. Communities, however, can make a difference. And importantly, they provide a distinctive social context within which individuals give support to and receive support from others. But what do we understand by 'community'?

What is community?

It is well established that contemporary lifestyles have brought with them a major shift in how we understand community and that the number of discrete communities that most of us belong to continues to increase. I don't have to go too far back in my family history, say to my grandparents' generation in the early years of the twentieth century, to find an example of a family whose community was easily described: their home and family lives, their working and worshipping communities all overlapped within a very small geographical area, because these were working-class people with few opportunities and still less desire to move away from the English south-coast town where they were all born and brought up.

A century later, I find myself part of a number of quite separate communities. There is no overlap at all between the village where I live, the church I attend ten miles away, and the job I commute to in central London, not to mention my family, most of whom live in a different part of the country altogether. Even within the village there are various separate, though overlapping, communities: the families who have always lived there; the people who regularly attend the village church; affluent people who have retired to the area and who busy themselves with forming daytime clubs and other social activities; regulars at the village pub; the allotment association; and people like me whose participation in any of these communities is confined to occasional attendance at church or pub and bursts of activity on my allotment. If there is such a thing as an overarching village community, I am a very marginal member of it.

Against this background, which is not untypical of life in the United Kingdom today, it makes little sense to talk simply of a local community or a church community unless we acknowledge that for most of us this is just one community among many. Yet we cling to the concept, inventing new communities for ourselves, which leads us to talk of such ill-defined (and probably non-existent) entities as 'the international community', 'the business community' and many more besides.

Yet this is not a wholly negative picture. Living as we do in a time of climate change crisis, it is imperative for communities, however they are defined, to get together with a common purpose. And this is perhaps more easily done today, with so many of us belonging to a range of different communities than would have been the case in my grandparents' day, although arguably they would have been much more accepting of external intervention, say of government control over their lives, than my generation is. In the absence of such acceptance, we need to look to our communities to be vehicles for change and to see the relationships between communities, locally, nationally and internationally, as our best hope for averting disaster.

The 'church community'

Let's focus now, though, on that area in people's lives that we define as 'church'. And while for most members of a church this is simply one community among many, it is worth bearing in mind that church life itself is also fragmented. The community that meets in a church building will have its own sub-groups: the youth group that meets on a Sunday evening; the committed activists (PCC members and the like); the (mainly older) people who come along to weekday services; mums and toddlers and similar church-based activities; and people within the church who get together outside it in their own interest groups – musicians, reading groups, football teams – not to mention home-based Bible study groups and so on. And then there are the inter-church structures that in turn form separate communities: members of local or national synods or other governing bodies; ecumenical networks that bring together members of different denominations; and the structures of related but external organisations such as mission or development agencies that create groups of church people sharing a passion for the church's work overseas.

How, then, should we define the church community? St Paul's characterisation of the church as the body of Christ in 1 Corinthians 12 is a splendid picture of oneness. In particular, the insight that when one part of the body suffers, all suffer, encourages church members to see themselves as integral to a much greater structure, characterised by their interdependence under Christ.

Yet the reality is far from this ideal. It is very hard to persuade people affected by HIV/AIDS in Africa or losing their homes to climate change-related disasters in Asia that the worldwide body of Christ is suffering with them. And Christians in the global North rarely suffer, even in a modest way, alongside their brothers and sisters in the South, unless they have themselves shared their experiences, at least temporarily. While a close-knit congregation in a single church may find the image of the body a helpful one in encouraging individuals' acceptance of one another, the feeling of interdependent community rapidly disappears once that community is extended beyond its immediately perceived bounds. Furthermore, the image of the church as Christ's body is not likely to be taken on board by its fringe members. And an essential part of defining a community surely has to do with how people perceive themselves.

Back in Chapter 3 I referred to Karl Barth's discussion of the 'life of the children of God'. Barth defines a community by its *commitment to take action*, and the Christian community by its willingness to undertake a specific type of action rooted in the command to love our neighbour. This is helpful in defining the characteristics of our disparate communities today and in bringing them together. For while all the mini communities that are somehow included in the idea of church may not see themselves as the deeply united whole that the Pauline idea of the body of Christ demands, they are brought together in action. Admittedly, the members of a church youth group may have an understanding of loving their neighbour that is rather different from that of the elderly mid-week congregation, which, in turn, differs from that of the ecumenical enthusiasts or the church football team. But they have in common a willingness to be active in their respective groups that is based on a shared rationale of treating their neighbour as themselves.

It is, I suggest, in this concept of community in action that hope lies when we are confronted with a global crisis such as climate change.

Communities and climate change

A community-based approach to climate change has both advantages and disadvantages, depending on the extent to which a community feels itself to be affected by global warming.

For example, the small rural village community of San Hilario in El Salvador, to the south-east of the capital San Salvador, is typical of many others in making concerted efforts to repair the damage done by the destruction of mangrove trees. Mangroves, described as 'the lungs of El Salvador', have been illegally cut down for the luxury furniture market, and have also been used by poor people for firewood. Yet the forests are vital in protecting people and land from the worst effects of flooding.

In this instance there is a clearly defined local community, its members well used to working together on common problems. Actions taken by individuals alone would be both ineffective and counter-cultural. And while this community has no capacity at all for reducing carbon emissions (because it is responsible for next to nothing in this respect), it is able to do something to reduce the effects of flooding in the aftermath of the increasing numbers of tropical storms and hurricanes.

But even when a community has a much greater capacity to bring about change than does the average group of Salvadorean farmers, it is wrong to assume that actions carried out within that community are a satisfactory response to climate change. And one fact that churches in particular in the developed world need to acknowledge is that community-centred action alone is not only largely ineffective; it all too easily breeds complacency.

A number of campaigns aimed at individuals in the UK have focused on the fact that people can make a difference. People are urged, quite rightly, not to leave their electrical equipment on standby, to use energy-saving light bulbs, to travel by bus or cycle rather than by car and by train rather than by air. Yet, as most people suspect, with the exception of that last detail, these things make very little difference to anything except one's own electricity bill. The same is true of most community action. However it is defined, the church community (or a school or workplace community) is pretty small, and changing the light bulbs is not going to halt the pace of global warming. And the danger in encouraging small actions together is a shared sense of complacency. People set themselves low targets and once these are achieved they tend to feel that they have reached the limit of the action that they individually and together can and should undertake. The answer is twofold: encourage actions outside the community and establish relationships between different forms of community to bring them about.

Relationships between communities: looking into the face of disaster

This is arguably one of the greatest challenges facing climate change campaigners today: how to get people to set their sights higher. In other words, how to encourage members of a community (or communities) to look outside that community for targets that will have greatest impact on the global warming crisis. For many people this will mean undertaking tasks they are not wholly comfortable with – for example, becoming political activists in order to lobby governments and key decision-makers about emissions targets. Yet here the community comes into its own, providing a base for action and encouragement for the wider engagement of its members.

But it is in relationships between communities that real hope is to be found. Which is stronger: a large impersonal online 'community' whose members have in common little more than their choice of website and a vague desire to be more 'green'; or groups of communities who share something much more deeply rooted? In the case of Christian communities, this is a belief in the Gospel of Jesus Christ; if relationships are extended further, to communities of people of other faiths, this becomes, more generally, a basis of religious conviction, with shared concerns for justice and for the well-being of their fellow human beings. The wider the network of relationships, the more powerful the communities become in pressing for change.

It is in relationships between communities that hope for the future is to be found. And it is here as well that true Christian hope lies. The Pauline image of the worldwide body of Christ may seem unrealistic to many, if not most, Christians. But groups of communities, all defined in Karl Barth's terms as united in actions carried out in obedience to love of one's neighbour, have both a conceptual and a very practical unity.

This means more than communities getting together to create a formidable body of opinion in public life. It demands that we keep the lawyer's question, 'Who is my neighbour?' constantly under review. My neighbour is not only a person in need within my own community or someone in close proximity. My neighbour – our neighbour – is also the whole of another community that is quite outside my own experience. Today's crisis demands that the community that is united by its actions of love shows that love to the communities of refugees in Bangladesh, to communities of rickshaw drivers forced out into the blazing sun of Delhi to scrape a living, to communities of poor farmers in El Salvador, replanting their mangrove swamps in the hope of staving off disaster. The survival of communities like these depends directly on the will of other communities. This means the will to bring about change through a dramatic reduction in carbon emissions in the industrialised global North; and the will to establish cross-community relationships and to offer practical love, by offering places of refuge, safe housing, renewable energy and so on.

Why do we find it so hard?

One thing churches are really good at is reinventing the wheel. Why we find it so important to devise our own tailor-made ways of responding to global warming, whether in liturgy or in practical action, instead of joining in with others, is a mystery that I do not propose to address here. Maybe the lingering fallacy that 'the Church can take a lead' has something to do with it: one group of people, one church, one diocese sees itself as spearheading a general 'Church' response to climate change, steams ahead regardless of all the other groups that are doing exactly the same thing, and then asks in wounded puzzlement why no one wants to join them.

This is unbiblical and, in the case of climate change, totally inappropriate. Faced with a global crisis, only as near a global response as possible is acceptable. That is why faith-based communities are so important: they are worldwide communities made up of local ones where every individual counts. That is the beauty of the Genesis Covenant idea. But which organisations will have the audacity to sign up to something they haven't devised themselves? That is the question.

Living with suffering

Our Christian response to suffering, whether as churches or as individuals, has to meet three basic criteria: it must be compassionate, proportionate and effective. Think of Jesus miraculously feeding the crowds who had gathered to listen to him. It all began because he had compassion on them after three days with nothing to eat (Mark 8:2). His response was in keeping with the size of the problem: he provided food for all of them. And it was effective – so much so that there were 12 baskets of food left over. We see the same pattern in Jesus' healing miracles: they begin with his compassion and there are no half measures in how he responds to people's needs.

Compassion

Compassion is not just feeling sorry for someone. Compassion means taking on someone else's suffering. And that means understanding both the nature and the cause of that suffering. People often complain that it is difficult to pray for people and situations they don't know. True enough, but it is not hard to find out. So compassion in a time of climate change depends firstly on the will to look and listen, to search out details in the press or via the internet and to reflect on what is happening to people and to the natural world.

An attitude of compassion is also a willing and unconditional response. Generosity is praised in the New Testament: Jesus singles out the gift of a poor widow to the Temple treasury (Luke 21:2–4) while, as Paul writes to Timothy, the rich are 'to do good, to be rich in good works, generous and ready to share' (1 Tim. 6:18). Yet how reluctant we are, by comparison, to give of our time, our talents or our wealth.

People often say that they like to see where their money is going or to have some say on how it is spent – a far cry from the widow who unconditionally gave 'all that she had to live on'. Our fragile earth, its biodiversity, its suffering people, demand nothing less.

Getting things in proportion

By any standards the behaviour of the poor widow was disproportionate. The Bible already sets high standards. The traditional tithe, giving away one tenth of one's income, is a demanding discipline, yet one that needs to be viewed in the light of the sacrificial giving of Jesus. Our compassion, like his, should set new levels of generosity for the Church and for ourselves. But it is also crucial that our response to people suffering injustice should be proportionate not to our means but to their needs and to the causes of their needs.

The climate change crisis has highlighted these factors in a deeply uncomfortable way. The injustice of the way in which global warming is affecting the poorest people has largely failed to evoke a significant compassionate response from the churches, let alone one which is proportionate to the size of the problem. While people die or are driven from their homes as a result of extreme weather, we are content with worthy but barely significant activities (installing low-energy light bulbs or sharing electric mowers) or even irrelevant ones (42 per cent of us apparently believe that recycling our rubbish will combat climate change). The argument that if, say, everyone used trains and buses, things would change, is unconvincing. There is little point in appealing to altruism in an essentially non-altruistic society.

A proportionate response to climate change lies elsewhere: in lobbying national and international bodies and demanding legislation that will force us to reduce our carbon emissions to a level that will seriously affect the lifestyles of all of us. We have to speak out and take action (Micah 6:8), and until the Church faces up to the full implications of what it means to 'do justice', it cannot claim to offer a lead in protecting the earth and its people.

Being effective

It follows from all this that the Church has to react to climate change in ways that are effective. There is no point in organising synod debates or setting up committees if these are not followed up by real action. But I suggest that there are two key ways in which the Church is uniquely placed to make an effective response.

The first suggestion is that the Church should recover its calling to be a servant. The teaching of Jesus that 'the Son of Man came not to be served but to serve' is not always easy to discern within the Church, which for some is a means of satisfying ambition and acquiring status. Liberation theology has shown us the way forward in empowering poor communities; but until it becomes the ambition of the churches in the North to stand together in an attitude of service with those in the South, our response to the people most vulnerable to climate change cannot hope to be fully effective.

My second suggestion is that, as already argued in Chapter 1, the Church should recover its prophetic voice. Despite the growth of secularism, people nationally and internationally still want to hear the ethical voice and see the moral leadership of the churches. Yet all too often that voice is silent, or else shows little understanding of today's world. An effective response to people's needs will reflect compassion and understanding, and in calling for action on the root causes of injustice it will deliver a clear message to the rich world.

Living the difference

Whether we like it or not (and I suspect many of us will like it), a low-carbon lifestyle will force us to slow down. Rising prices and a move away from pre-packaged food will change our eating habits; oil shortages will reduce our travel options; home working and other flexible working options should add to our leisure time. And while most Christians are probably as fond as anyone else of their takeaway coffees and multitasking on their Blackberrys, there is a theological imperative for a more measured way of life.

Barth's covenant theology emphasises the importance of the Sabbath, which he sees as the end of the work of creation and the beginning of the covenant relationship between God and humankind. The goal of creation, says Barth, is 'Sabbath freedom, Sabbath rest and Sabbath joy', and this is not restricted to God alone but shared with humankind: 'Man is created to participate in this [Sabbath] rest before any human activity.'[4] So human beings alone share in God's creation and also in God's rest.

Recovering rest or leisure is a necessary – and pleasurable – part of living with global warming. But we need to be clear what we mean by leisure. It is not just the absence of work, any more than peace is just the absence of conflict. Both leisure and peace are positive things. And leisure enables human creativity and sociability to develop in ways that genuinely complement our working lives. So leisure is neither an extension of work nor a complete shutting down of our infinitely varied human gifts and abilities.

What does all this mean for someone like Bono, quoted at the start of this chapter, who is in some way representative of all of us whose livelihoods, and indeed whose 'good works', depend on jetting round the world? It would of course be wrong of me to prescribe solutions for other people that I am unwilling or unable to adopt myself. But I would suggest that all our working lives are on the brink of becoming very different, with carbon-intensive travel and so on likely to be the exception rather than the rule. We need to focus our talents locally and let technology do the rest, with live appearances in a different part of the world being something to be specially valued. The risk with that, of course, is that the celebrity, or even the preacher, once seen in the flesh will prove to be something of a disappointment!

Silence in heaven

The Book of Revelation provides two sets of images of environmental devastation, in chapters 8 and 16. The death of vegetation, the collapse of mountains and the loss of animal life (8:7–9), followed by water pollution and atmospheric upheaval (8:10–12), are all heralded by the angels with trumpets. And these disasters are close enough to those faced by a world that is heating up to send shivers down the spine. But there is still time: John's vision allows space for repentance, before the 'bowls of wrath' are finally poured out in chapter 16.

There is here both warning and hope. But the point I want to stress is that the warning is one of total destruction. Our repentance, our response, must be in proportion to what lies ahead of us if we are to avoid a catastrophe similar to that described in Revelation 18. A small, measured response, just in case, will not do. Christian living in a time of global warming means an appropriate and proportionate way of doing things. Understanding that this is the case and changing the way we live (which is repentance by any other name) is where the hope of all of us is to be found.

Questions for discussion

1. What do you consider to be an appropriate response to global warming (a) by the worldwide Church and (b) by the local church community?

2. What actions on climate change has your church taken in the past year? Could this have been done more effectively with other churches or organisations? How do you plan to develop your work in the future?

Chapter 8

Where Does Christian Hope Lie?

Earth was heaven a little worse for wear. And heaven was
earth, done up again to look like new.

Wilkie Collins, *The Moonstone* (1868)

The religious enthusiast's view of heaven and earth in Collins's novel could be said to be somewhat lacking in imagination. Yet if we understand John's vision of a new heaven and a new earth in Revelation 21 as a promise for our time and for our world, it is perhaps not so wide of the mark. The challenge for the Church in a time of global warming is to offer hope, in the form of healing for the earth, an earth which by virtue of its redeemed nature will indeed resemble heaven, albeit a little worse for wear.

A new heaven and a new earth
(Rev. 21:1–8)

The precise nature of John's 'new earth' and how it will come into being has, unsurprisingly, been much debated and has been subject to changing interpretation. The first two verses of Revelation 21 suggest not so much a transformation or re-creation as a dramatic substitution of new for old. Yet God's proclamation, 'See, I am making all things new' (v. 5), does appear to indicate an evolution: the old is regenerated, given new life. That process is replicated in people's lives: the thirsty will have water, not any old thirst-quencher but 'a gift from the spring of the water of life' (v. 6). There is both physical and spiritual renewal, with the new emerging out of the old. Yet all this comes at a cost: those hostile to the new order receive a very public punishment. And at the top of the list are the cowards, Christians who did not accept the martyrdom for which the churches at Smyrna, Pergamum and Sardis have been commended.

Medieval monasticism saw life in the New Jerusalem as a monastic-style community – heaven on earth. And while we may no longer subscribe to the ideal of William Blake to build Jerusalem in 'England's green and pleasant land', we should not reject out of hand the role of human beings in helping to bring about transformation. At the same time, the sea – symbol of human excess in its association with the traders of Babylon – is no more (v. 1). We are witnessing a new way of living in a regenerated world.

Hope, then, lies in change. And while it is ultimately God who enables the earth he created to be renewed, thanks to his gift to us of a creation that contains within it the seeds of its own regeneration, that change depends on human beings co-operating with the process of renewal. Part of that co-operation lies in our readiness to heal our relationships with one another, to come together as community, as suggested in Chapter 7. And part of it too is in repairing our relationship with the natural world, halting the activities and processes that we know to be damaging.

Revelation 21 offers us a vision for a future which may not be as distant as we think. Its verses represent a hope that we can celebrate in worship and that we can cling to in times of setback and opposition. But in the Gospels we have also a hope for every day. There we find hope not for our future but for our present in the assurance of Jesus' resurrection and how we are called to live in the light of that. So while there is in Revelation 21 a glimpse of what the future will be like if we take up the challenge of restoring and renewing the earth, the Gospels themselves will guide us in our efforts to work towards that renewal.

The resurrection commands of Jesus

Action is a key message of the resurrection. The Gospel accounts of Jesus' resurrection appearances have, mostly, a twofold purpose. First and foremost they convey the information that Jesus has risen from the dead. But, secondly, there is a command to act: feed my lambs (John 21:15), go and make disciples (Matt. 28:19), forgive people's sins (John 20:23). The hope of the resurrection is not something that we can keep to ourselves: we must pass it on to others by doing whatever is necessary to address their needs. This is all summed up in Jesus' final words to his disciples in Luke's Gospel, after he had explained how Scripture had been ful-filled in him: 'You are witnesses of these things' (Luke 24:48). The gift of the Holy Spirit would enable those witnesses to speak and act accordingly, as the Acts of the Apostles duly records that they did.

'Go and make disciples of all nations' (Matt. 28:19)

In all that I have heard and read about climate change and the Church, there is one fundamental question that I must have missed. Quite simply it's this: what does the Church do best – and how is it going to keep on doing it in a world under threat from global warming?

Although I have said a lot about the Church speaking out, about learning to love our neighbour and so on, like others, I have not so far touched upon the reason for the Church's very existence, which is enshrined in Jesus' great commission at the end of Matthew's Gospel. The Church's calling is to do mission, to make disciples of all nations. That is what the Church does best; that is what no other institution in the world can do for it. So following on from the previous chapter, where I suggested that we should look at how we live in a time of global warming, I want to ask the question, what does the mission of the Church look like in a time of environmental crisis? Because if we do not address that question, if we do not phrase it in those terms, I believe there is a very real possibility that the mission of the Church will be destroyed.

There is a certain fallacy that is vigorously alive in many UK churches that talks about doing mission by example. If I live a good life and go to church on Sundays, the argument goes, other people will want to do the same. I don't need to embarrass myself or my friends by talking about my faith or by asking them to come along to church with me. It will simply happen.

This is of course no model for mission. It is no coincidence that the churches that are currently growing are those whose members have the courage and the faith to go out and talk to people, to risk embarrassment, to devise new ways of encouraging people to find out about Christianity. And in much the same way, silent example is no model for sustainable living in a world that is warming up. While I suspect that many Christians would find it easier to talk to their neighbours about carbon emissions than about the Gospel, I cannot delude myself that if I put solar panels on my roof and don't bother telling anyone why, my neighbours will all rush to do the same. Neither the Church as an institution, nor we who make up the Church, can rely on silent example to do either our work of Christian mission or our task of addressing climate change for us.

So what is our Christian mission to look like, not in the future, but right now as the world heats up? While this probably deserves a book in itself, it seems to me that our changing context should be reflected in the following: our theology and evangelism – the message of hope, of a new earth – which in turn influences our preaching, teaching and worship; our outreach and pastoral care, most particularly to people least able to cope with change; our concern for justice and development; and our lives, whether in ministry or as lay members of the Christian community.

This reflects the 'five marks of mission' developed by the Anglican Consultative Council for the worldwide Anglican Communion in the late 1980s:

- to proclaim the Good News of the Kingdom;
- to teach, baptise and nurture new believers;
- to respond to human need by loving service;
- to seek to transform unjust structures of society;
- to strive to safeguard the integrity of creation and sustain and renew the life of the earth.

Theology

The interdependence of people on one another and on the created world can no longer be regarded as just a theoretical concept. We can see it for ourselves, as plant and animal life changes before our eyes as the result of human activity, as people suffer from floods, drought, famine and other disasters. To this interdependence Christian theology adds the dependence of all of us on God and the hope that is given us through our oneness with him.

This is the message of hope (already outlined) that it is our mission to proclaim. We take hope too from the promise of forgiveness and healing. In a world which risks being brought to its knees (metaphorically speaking) by materialistic excesses, the promise of forgiveness for our part in that and the realistic hope of a new and different world are both crucially important. And, I believe, both are very attractive to believers and non-believers alike.

The outworking of this in worship does not condemn us to a lifetime of hymns about the beauty of the earth, where every Sunday is Environment Sunday, or every season in the liturgical year is Creation Time. Rather, our commitment to 'safeguard the integrity of creation' should lead us to reflect on our oneness with our fellow human beings and with God, to an acknowledgement of the shared suffering of creation and of humanity, and to a determination under God to address it.

Reflecting biblically on creation and the climate change crisis is a necessary part of that commitment. But we should not be putting our efforts into hunting out all the references in the Bible to the natural world and struggling to get them to 'fit' our current situation. Rather, we should consider the bottom-up approach to biblical texts as pioneered by liberation theologians back in the 1960s, and ask the question, how do we, as people living in a time of environmental danger, understand this or that passage?

In preaching on poverty and justice issues, I have come back time and again to Matthew 25:31–46: Jesus' teaching on the separation of the righteous and the unrighteous, on the basis of their response to people in great need, with the wonderful assurance, 'just as you did it to one of the least of these who are members of my family, you did it to me' (v. 40). How now are we to understand that? Just as you gave up damaging the atmosphere with your carbon emissions, just as you called for improved farming methods, just as you sought to protect biodiversity – there is almost infinite variety in today's forms of righteousness or unrighteousness.

Romans 13 is another passage that proves illuminating in the light of climate change. 'Be subject to the governing authorities' (v. 1) – that is, be faithful in observing environmental laws and regulations, don't try to find a way round them, and pay whatever environmental taxes come your way (v. 7). 'Love does no wrong to a neighbour' (v. 10) sums up all that I have been saying thus far about the injustice of global warming and how we must go about restoring justice. And 'now is the time for you to wake from sleep' (v. 11) again speaks for itself, given the urgency of our current situation.

If we are serious about living Christian lives in a rapidly changing environmental context, this will necessarily be reflected in our worship and reflection. And we shall be the richer for it.

Local outreach

Considering the mission of the Church in a time of global warming does not require a great leap of imagination, although a certain amount of lateral thinking may be in order. It looks as though one of the main impacts on the UK will be an increase in heavy rain and flooding, and this would be a good starting point for churches in vulnerable areas. Outreach is of course much more than the local vicar, bishop or archbishop being photographed in his or her wellies alongside people whose homes have flooded. I suggest it means things like ongoing support for people living in temporary accommodation, practical help in dealing with insurance companies or social security, help with small repairs, working with the media to keep the difficulties of both urban and rural communities in the spotlight, and much more besides. With the after-effects of floods lasting not for weeks but for months or even years, local churches will be in it for the long haul, not just for media opportunities in the first week.

Outreach means helping people prepare for disaster as well as coping with it afterwards. This may be as basic as having a list of things to do when flooding is forecast posted prominently in a church or community centre. It may sound alarmist, but it is common sense, as anyone who has worked in disaster risk reduction in developing countries will tell you.

We need to remember too that extreme weather means loss of livelihoods, especially for people who are self-employed. This might range from the paperboy or -girl who can't get out of the house to do a paper round, to a businessperson whose equipment is destroyed. And as always, it is people dependent on the land who will suffer most. In the future everyone should be able to find practical help and advice freely available from their local church community.

Then there are opportunities for mission in hitherto unforeseen areas. I live near the Oxford–Banbury canal, and I was intrigued to read of a plan by major road haulage companies to use waterways as an alternative to the roads, thereby saving on oil costs and carbon emissions. What will the local churches in Oxfordshire be doing, I wonder, to welcome this extra traffic through our parishes? Good refreshment facilities and informal evening or Sunday worship would seem to be the very least we could offer.

I am taking it as read that local congregations will be doing all they can to address their own carbon footprint. But in a few years' time, many of our potentially carbon-burning activities will be controlled by legislation. The faithful observance of laws that are intended for nature to be healed will become our Christian responsibility, and the Church needs to be vociferous in its support for regulation. At the same time, though, we need to remember my earlier point about the middle-class nature of environmental protection and controls. Local churches should surely make it their business to be aware of the impact of environmental legislation on people least able to afford it, and to offer appropriate help and support.

Crossing borders

The inevitable disasters that global warming will continue to cause will make unparalleled demands on Christians' support for their brothers and sisters overseas, mainly but not exclusively in the developing countries. This demands of us that we honour our belief in the nature of the Church as the body of Christ. St Paul's statement in 1 Corinthians 12 that 'If one member [of the body] suffers, all suffer together with it' is a principle to which we tend to pay no more than lip service. What does it mean to suffer with our homeless brothers and sisters in South-East Asia? What does it mean to feel the pain of farmers in sub-Saharan Africa whose land has dried up and whose animals have died? What does it mean to share the bereavement of people who have lost family members to cyclones and floods in Central America?

These are questions that in a time of global warming we must be able to answer. Our church communities need to get themselves better informed about what is going on. We need to pray constantly – and imaginatively – for the people affected. We need to be generous with our money in responding to emergency needs and generous with our time in exploring how best we can support the suffering members of our worldwide Church.

Pastoral care

Responding to human need is a key part of Christian life and also a complicated one. At the level most of us undertake it, though, it is an instinctive and largely unskilled task. It does not require a course in pastoral care to know when to give someone who is upset a hug or when to get out your rods and sort out an elderly neighbour's blocked drain. But the danger is always that, given the presence of trained pastors, we abdicate that basic care to the professionals. Climate change will make those basic human demands of all of us.

At a deeper level, though, there are people's hopes and fears in the face of global warming. Are we and our pastors properly equipped to answer the awkward questions on the future of the planet which may be tormenting a young person? Are we able to respond to the anger of a bereaved parent who has lost a son or daughter in a climate-related disaster? Global warming has implications not only for the quality of our pastoral care but for the training of our carers.

It would also be unrealistic to assume that climate-related disaster will never strike our own particular neck of the woods. Being ill prepared to offer care in an emergency is likely to result in inadequate pastoral care. Again there are implications for training our pastors, which should be addressed sooner rather than later. Plenty of people know the theory about stages of grief after bereavement. I wonder how many of them can also handle questions like 'Why is nature punishing me?' without denying the goodness of God the Creator.

Church structures

One thing that I have learnt over many years working with and for the Church, whether locally, nationally or internationally, is that its structures are rather inadequate when it comes to coping with the demands of modern life. This is another topic which it would not be appropriate to explore in any detail here, but we do need to ask the question: what structures need to be changed (or perhaps better, what structures do we need to have in place) in the Church in a time of global warming?

In general, cumbersome structures are not well suited to urgent situations. And to adhere to a system that is by definition slow – such as the Anglican synodical structure, whereby the outcomes from debates in the national General Synod have to be fed down through debates in Diocesan Synods, then Deanery Synods, before they reach parish level – is to undermine the urgency of addressing the climate change crisis and is, in my view, insulting to those suffering its effects. So there needs to be a way of doing things that gets more or less instant buy-in from people at all levels of representation in the Church – an obvious case for the better use of electronic communications.

Naturally a structure which obviates the need for people to travel to meetings, often from quite a distance, is environmentally preferable as well as being more efficient. I have tried – and failed – to convince international bodies of that. But from a purely economic point of view, the money saved on international flights to Christian conferences could be much better spent on permanent telecommunications technology instead.

At a more local level we should also consider the way in which our human resources are structured. Does every diocese need an environmental adviser? Would it not be more effective to train diocesan missioners, trainers, pastors, building committees and so on in what it means to be a church in a time of global warming? This would enable climate change to be effectively mainstreamed across all areas of church life, and remove the perception that it is a specialist interest.

And finally, a plea for a joined-up approach. Like all big organisations, the Church's right hand risks not knowing (or caring) what its left hand is doing. I have several times been in the curious situation of listening to a leading clergy figure argue passionately that the Church can take a lead on combating climate change, while looking out at the local cathedral lit up like a Christmas tree in the summer twilight.

Christian living

Good lives don't have to cost the earth. That is the conclusion of a book by a wide range of authors, from politicians to chefs, to novelists and philosophers. In their concluding essay, the editors, Joe Smith and Andrew Simms, re-state their premise: 'Achieving a good life for more than six billion people, without further threatening the ecological systems on which we all depend, is the greatest challenge of our age.' And their conclusion, given that 'there are so many ways in which our dominant measures of personal and economic success are incomplete', is that good lives offer our best chance of preserving the earth.[1]

What is a good life? On a purely utilitarian basis it is not to be equated with wealth, because research has shown that people's happiness does not increase with their income. For Philip Pullman, a contributor to the same book, it is a combination of a life that is pleasant and satisfying and one that is 'full of moral purpose'.[2] I guess for most of us who are Christians the former is a consequence of the latter, though few of us, even the most ascetic, would deliberately opt for an unpleasant life. And for 'moral purpose' we would want to say a life lived in accordance with God's will.

So what does Christian living mean in a time of global warming? I suggest that, above all, it is a life based on healed relationships, in the sense explored in previous chapters. It is a life lived in a good relationship with the natural world – from which flow all the familiar 'green' activities like buying local food or growing your own, saving energy and opting for renewables, and so on. It is also a life lived in a good relationship with our neighbours, and that includes supporting our neighbours who are vulnerable to extreme weather on the other side of the world, as well as offering practical help locally (if you live in a vulnerable area yourself) and speaking out about the urgent need to cut carbon emissions.

The church at Smyrna: riches, affliction and poverty (Rev. 2:8–11)

The church in the ancient city of Smyrna was beset by the same danger as the church in Philadelphia: violent persecution instigated by local Jews. While John recognises that such actions are untrue to Judaism, he describes their activity in both cases as satanic opposition, referring to the 'synagogue of Satan' (v. 9). And more danger is imminent. John warns of 'ten days' of affliction, probably a relatively short time rather than a period of indeterminate length that, say, the more usual mystical number seven might suggest.

But there is great hope in the message to Smyrna, with its explicit promise of 'the crown of life' (v. 11). This is no less than the resurrection hope that is alluded to in verse 8: 'These are the words of the first and the last, who was dead and came to life.' This was strangely appropriate to Smyrna's history. The original Greek city had been destroyed in the seventh century BC and was not rebuilt for another four centuries. Then the city was reborn, and had a claim to be the first city of Asia.

The worldwide Church today is set in an environmental context which may or may not be reborn. Like the seven churches of Revelation, our local churches are called to live appropriately in a non-Christian setting and to resist any compromise with non-Christian values. The hope of rebirth has been set before us. It is up to us whether or not we engage with the difficult but not insuperable challenge of bringing that about: a choice of life or death, both physical and spiritual.

Questions for discussion

1. What actions can you and your church take that will offer real hope to the people most affected by global warming?
2. Imagine your local community in ten years' time. How will it have been affected by climate change and what difference will this make to your church's outreach to local people?

Notes

Chapter 1: The Time Is Near

1. Gill Ereaut and Nat Sgnit, *Warm Words: How are we telling the climate story and can we tell it better?* (IPPR, 2006), available at www.ippr.org
2. It is important to remember that climate change is as much subject to media 'spin' as any other area of life today. Oxford University's Environmental Change Institute is engaged in a study of the influence of the media on climate science and policy and the public, which will explore how the media affects public understanding of the causes and consequences of climate change. See www.eci.ox.ac.uk/research/climate/massmedia.php
3. UNFCC stands for the United Nations Framework Convention on Climate Change.
4. 'Forests First in the Fight Against Climate Change', May 2007.
5. IPCC Fourth Assessment Report, Working Group III, Summary for Policymakers, 2007, p. 2.
6. Reported in The *Guardian*, 12 May 2008.
7. Ibid. The article quotes Martin Parry, co-chair of the IPCC: 'Levels of greenhouse gases continue to rise in the atmosphere and the rate of that rise is accelerating. We are already seeing the impacts of climate change and the scale of those impacts will also accelerate, until we decide to do something about it.'
8. Interview in The *Guardian*, 7 April 2008.
9. Source: Indian Meteorology Institute.
10. Source: Instituto Nacional de Recursos Naturales, glaciology unit.

11. Source: New Economics Foundation, *Africa – Up in Smoke?* (2005), p. 19.
12. Source: Christian Aid, *The Climate of Poverty* (May 2006), p. 30.
13. Christian Aid, internal communication.
14. Various contributors at the UNFCCC 13th Conference of Parties, Bali, December 2007.
15. Expressed, for example, by Judith Kovacs and Christopher Roland in *Revelation* (Oxford, Blackwell Publishing, 2004).

Chapter 2: False Prophets

1. Details reported by the BBC Environment correspondent Richard Black, ' "No sun link" to climate change', 3 April 2008, available at http://news.bbc.co.uk/l/hi/sci/tech/7327393.stm
2. *An Appeal to Reason: A Cool Look at Global Warming* (Duckworth, 2008).
3. *The Stern Review on the Economics of Climate Change* (HM Treasury, 30 October 2006).
4. 'Faith and the Future of the Earth', downloadable from the Diocese of Liverpool website, www.liverpool.anglican.org from the section 'Bishop James' speeches'.
5. Source: Greenpeace China, communication from Li Yan, climate and energy campaigner, 30 June 2008.
6. www.amityfoundation.org and personal communication.
7. The St George's lecture, 1 June 2007, entitled 'Faith and the Future of the Earth'. This is downloadable from the Diocese of Liverpool website, www.liverpool.anglican.org from the section 'Bishop James' speeches'.

Chapter 3: The Injustice of Climate Change

1. December 2007.
2. *Scivias* I and ii.10.7, quoted in Judith Kovacs and Christopher Roland, *Revelation* (Oxford, Blackwell Publishing, 2004), p. 57.
3. Estimate by the Dutch agency Kerkinactie in 2006.
4. Evo Morales, President of Bolivia, addressing the United Nations in April 2008.
5. Interim report of the Special Rapporteur on the right to food, Jean Zigler, submitted to the UN General Assembly, 22 August 2007.
6. Christian Aid, *Fighting food shortages: hungry for change* (July 2008).
7. The outcome of our discussions is reflected in my paper, 'Theology and the HIV/AIDS epidemic' (Christian Aid, 2004). David has explored Barthian ideas of covenant and creation in relation to climate change much more fully than I am able to do here in *Renewing the face of the earth: a theological and pastoral response to climate change* (SCM/ Canterbury Press, 2008).
8. Karl Barth, translated by J.W. Edwards, O. Bussey and H. Knight, *Church Dogmatics* III, 1: 'The Doctrine of Creation' (Edinburgh, T. & T. Clark, 1955).
9. Details from the International Council for Human Rights Policy, *Rights and climate change* (draft seen March 2008), pp. 33–4.
10. Institute of Development Studies (University of Sussex), 'We know what we need: South Asian women speak out on climate change adaptation', *ActionAid*, November 2007.
11. Position paper, December 2007.
12. Madame Pélagie Simbinuba, a Mothers' Union worker in Matana, Burundi.
13. Muna Mukeri, Banke, Nepal, quoted in Institute of Development Studies (University of Sussex), 'We know what we need', op. cit.

Chapter 4: The Right to Live

1. Jürgen Moltmann, *On Human Dignity: Political Theology and Ethics* (English translation, SCM Press, 1984), p. 17.
2. Ibid., p. 15.
3. Ibid., p. 27.
4. Internal Christian Aid report, May 2006.
5. Interim report of the Special Rapporteur on the right to food, Jean Zigler, submitted to the UN General Assembly, 22 August 2007.
6. Scott Fields, *Environmental Health Perspectives*, Vol. 113, No. 8 (August 2005), quoted in Christian Aid, *The Climate of Poverty* (May 2006), p. 9.
7. Christian Aid, *The Climate of Poverty*, op. cit., p. 10.
8. *The Risen Christ and the Eucharistic World* (1972, English translation: Collins, 1976), p. 36 (original emphasis).
9. Ibid., p. 39.
10. Set out in *Church Dogmatics*, translated by J.W. Edwards, O. Bussey and H. Knight (Edinburgh, T. & T. Clark, 1955), I,2.
11. Available online at www.ciwf.org
12. Darton Longman and Todd (2007), p. 256.
13. For more detailed information see, for example, *Indigenous Affairs*, issue 1-2/08, on 'Climate change and indigenous peoples' (published by the International Work Group for Indigenous Affairs, Copenhagen, website www.iwgia.org).
14. The Anglican solitary Maggie Ross has done much to make the spirituality of the Arctic peoples more widely known. See, for example, 'The walrus of the living God' in *Weavings*, 23(5) (2008), pp. 16–22.

Chapter 5: Trade, Development and Conservation

1. Thanks to Andrew Simms of the new economics foundation for this memorable calculation.
2. 'Summary of conclusions' (HM Treasury, 30 October 2006), p. viii.

3. See their first report, *A Green New Deal* (new economics foundation, July 2008), ISBN 978 1 904882 35 0.
4. There is more information on GDRs at www.ecoequity.org
5. 'Pro-Poor Climate Change Adaptation: A Research Agenda', *In Focus*, 02.2 (November 2007).
6. Hannah Reid and David Satterthwaite, 'Climate change and cities: why urban agendas are central to adaptation and mitigation' (IIED, December 2007).
7. From Paula Clifford, 'The human face of ecotheology: how far can we go', in *Økoteologi* (Trondheim, Tapir Akademisk Forlag, 2007), pp. 179–88.

Chapter 6: An Open Door

1. From Christian Aid, *Human tide: the real migration crisis* (May 2007).
2. IPCC Fourth Assessment Report, chapter 20.
3. Quoted in Christian Aid, *Human tide: the real migration crisis* (May 2007), p. 25.
4. The website of the Optimum Population Trust has a ticking 'population clock': see www.optimumpopulation.org
5. Quoted in Paul Vallely, 'Population paradox: Europe's time bomb', The *Independent* (9 August 2008).

Chapter 7: Living with Global Warming

1. Rock star and anti-poverty campaigner Bono talking about the problems of reducing personal carbon emissions (28 January 2008 at the World Economic Forum in Davos).
2. Parts of this chapter draw on my article 'Communities, Theology and Climate Change' published in the Taiwan-based journal *Theologies and Cultures*, Vol. 4, No. 1 (June 2007), pp. 48–58, and also on my chapter

entitled 'Hope for the poorest of the world' in Adrian Alker (ed.), *Together in Hope* (Sheffield, St Mark's CRC Press, 2008).

3. *The Revelation of St John the Divine* (London, A. & C. Black, 2nd edn, 1968), p. 47.
4. Karl Barth, *Church Dogmatics*, III/1 (1945), 'The Doctrine of Creation', translated by J.W. Edwards, O. Bussey and H. Knight (Edinburgh, T. & T. Clark, 1958), p. 98.

Chapter 8: Where Does Christian Hope Lie?

1. Andrew Simms and Joe Smith (eds.), *Do good lives have to cost the earth?* (Constable, 2008), p. 242.
2. Philip Pullman, in Simms and Smith (eds.), *Do good lives have to cost the earth?*, op. cit., p. 62.